Work Positive in a Negative World
The Team Edition

Praise for *Work Positive in a Negative World*

"*Work Positive in a Negative World* is about power, action and principle. It's helpful, and most of all, paradigm shifting. In our always-on, negative oriented media culture, Dr. Joey's book is a gift. Read it and change your work life for the better."

—**Tim Sanders**, author of *Today We Are Rich*

"Read Dr. Joey's *Work Positive in a Negative World* and discover how to be one of those rare people that creates happiness wherever they go. If you do, you'll be labeled a big thinker and get to chart your own course."

—**Michael Port**, author of *Book Yourself Solid*

"To apply the strategies in this book is to dramatically improve your business and life—period. Dr. Joey's insights into how to *Work Positive in a Negative World* provide a powerfully effective blueprint for achieving higher levels of success in all areas of your life, to the point where others will be specifically seeking you out because they want the chance to network with you!"

—**Dr. Ivan Misner**, *New York Times* bestselling author and founder of BNI, the world's largest business networking organization

"This book shows you how to unleash and channel your positive energy to get more done, better and faster than you ever thought possible."

—**Brian Tracy**, author of *How the Best Leaders Lead*

"If you want wisdom, truth and motivation to achieve your dreams, then listen to Dr. Joey. His words will help you soar!"

—**Rochelle Riley**, nationally syndicated columnist and author of *Raising A Parent*

"Every page of this book is an 'aha' experience and helps the reader find his or her own solutions to their daily challenges. You must buy, read and absorb this book and if you really desire success in life, buy some extra copies for your family, boss and work colleagues. You'll be doing yourself a huge favor!"

—**Mike Podolinsky**, CSP, Singapore Asia's Productivity Guru

"Dr. Joey's five core practices and the stories he tells in *Work Positive in a Negative World* make it easy to improve your attitude which determines your altitude and the impact you have on others."

—**Hugh F. Gouldthorpe Jr.**, author of *I've Always Looked Up to Giraffes* and *How to Make A Giraffe Smile*

work
positive
in a negative world

THE **TEAM** EDITION

redefine your reality and
achieve your work dreams

dr. joey faucette

NEW YORK

LONDON • NASHVILLE • MELBOURNE • VANCOUVER

Work Positive in a Negative World, The Team Edition

Redefine Your Reality and Achieve Your Work Dreams

Published in New York, New York, by Morgan James Publishing. Morgan James is a trademark of Morgan James, LLC. www.MorganJamesPublishing.com

This publication is designed to provide accurate and authoritative information in regard to the subject matter covered. It is sold with the understanding that the publisher is not engaged in rendering legal, accounting or other professional services. If legal advice or other expert assistance is required, the services of a competent professional person should be sought.

Givers Gain® is a registered trademark, and has been reproduced with permission of BNI Enterprises, Inc.

Work Positive ® is a registered trademark of Listen to Life, Too LLC.

Scripture marked NKJV is taken from the New King James Version®. Copyright © 1982 by Thomas Nelson. Used by permission. All rights reserved.

Proudly distributed by Ingram Publisher Services.

Morgan James BOGO™

A **FREE** ebook edition is available for you or a friend with the purchase of this print book.

[ ]

CLEARLY SIGN YOUR NAME ABOVE

Instructions to claim your free ebook edition:
1. Visit MorganJamesBOGO.com
2. Sign your name CLEARLY in the space above
3. Complete the form and submit a photo of this entire page
4. You or your friend can download the ebook to your preferred device

ISBN 9781631951350 paperback
ISBN 9781631951367 eBook
Library of Congress Control Number:
2020936286

Interior Design by:
Chris Treccani
www.3dogcreative.net

Author Photo:
Alice Abbott Photography

Morgan James is a proud partner of Habitat for Humanity Peninsula and Greater Williamsburg. Partners in building since 2006.

Get involved today! Visit: www.morgan-james-publishing.com/giving-back

To Briar Anne Shelton, my first grandchild,
who teaches me how to team in a whole new way

Contents

Thank you for purchasing the *Work Positive in a Negative World: The Team Edition* book. Download these bonuses that further empower you to create a Work Positive culture. Scan the QR code to get yours now!

- **Work Positive Checklist** – a simple checklist that coaches you to attract top talent and reduce team turnover.
- **Work Positive 5 Core Practices Cheat Sheet** – use this easy-to-follow guide to implement the 5 habit-sets of the Work Positive framework.
- **Work Positive Grab & Go Inspirations** – quick read positive thoughts to start your day in the best mindset.
- **Work Positive Affirmations** – begin each day the Work Positive way. Listen as Dr. Joey shares positive affirmations to focus on the positive and filter out the negative.

Also, join the Work Positive Community. Each of the "Consider How You Work Positive . . . " coaching box questions in this book are topics in the Work Positive Community online. You get a free membership with this book. Answer the questions online, learn from others' answers, and comment on them. Learn from the Work Positive Community how you can create a positive work culture that increases productivity and profits. Scan the QR code at the top of the page to set up your free account.

For many of you, ***Work Positive in a Negative World: Team Edition*** will present a process of waking up the dreams of work you had as a child. The mergers, downsizing, firings, forced retirement, global pandemics and other forms of unexpected change in the workplace in the last few years have served as a clarion wake-up call for dreams that had gone dormant. Many of you have been given the opportunity to take a fresh look at "Is this really the work I was born to do?" In these pages, Dr. Joey provides a plan for the 67% to 75% of you who describe yourselves as "disconnected and dissatisfied" at work. Yes, you can Work Positive.

The moment you express a desire for something more than repetitive, meaningless work, something more than simply punching the clock and realize that meaningful, purposeful, and profitable work really is a possibility, is the moment you've already taken an important step toward reawakening the dreams and passions you may have had as a child. All of a sudden, complacency and "comfortable misery" become intolerable. The idea of putting your calling on the shelf becomes intolerable. Not only do you have the opportunity, you have the responsibility of spending your working hours in work that will elevate you to your highest calling and transform the world around you.

I was raised on a dairy farm in rural Ohio. My father was a farmer and the pastor of one the two small churches in our one-caution-light town, which gave me a unique perspective on the world. Fulfilling God's will meant honoring my father and mother, attending church at least three times a week, not swearing like my town buddies, and keeping my word. Going to ball games, swimming pools, proms, dances, and having free time were out. Work was a constant, seven-days-a-week activity. Cows needed to be milked twice a day, 365 days a year. Corn needed to be planted, hay needed to be mowed, and chicken coops needed to be cleaned.

But wait a minute. Isn't that what growing up is all about? Doesn't every responsible person forget about dreams and passions in exchange for getting a paycheck? Absolutely not! Let me assure you that it doesn't need to be this way at all. Each of us, no matter what age we are or what kind of work we're doing now, can learn to bring the same excitement to our work that we experienced as a child at play. I believe each of us can pursue work that is a reflection of our best selves—a true application of our calling in life.

Despite the limitations on the things I could do or the places I could go as a poor farm kid, nothing could stop my mind from wandering. I remember well driving our little Ford tractor out in the fields, far away from anyone else, giving me time to imagine a world I had never seen. Somehow in that restricted world, when I was about twelve years old, I was able to get a copy of the little 33.3 rpm record by Earl Nightingale titled *The Strangest Secret*. On that recording I heard this gravelly voiced man say that I could be anything I wanted to be by simply changing my thinking. He talked about six words that could dramatically affect the results of my best efforts: **"We become what we think about."** I recognized if that were true, the possibilities of what I could do with my life were limitless.

While this is a biblical principle ("As a man thinks in his heart, so is he." NKJV) I knew my expectations for that phrase would not be welcomed in our house. My dad would not see that as an acceptable method for seeing and having more than what our simple farming life offered. After all, *we're just a passin' through* and wanting more opened the door to the dangers of moving away from contentment and basic godliness. I hid that little record under my mattress, bringing it out night after night to listen, dream and imagine. And I started to plan what my life could look like if in fact my thinking led the way. Any sense of being trapped began to disappear as I saw my opportunity, and responsibility, for the direction of my life.

If all you're looking for in work is a guaranteed paycheck, medical benefits, workmen's compensation, fringe benefits and a retirement plan, you may miss finding your Work Positive. Don't miss your opportunity to find or create work that is a blend of your talents, dreams and spiritual calling. It's an accepted stance to hate our jobs and to belittle the boss and the company, while patting ourselves on the back for being "responsible providers" for ourselves and families. Give up your freedom and you'll have two cars in the garage, a fine house, a nice vacation once a year, and you will no longer have to suffer the agony of choice.

I challenge you to accept the opportunity you're being given to move into your Work Positive. Walk through these core practices to Work Positive: Perceive, Conceive, Believe, Achieve, and Receive.

Recognize the freedom we have to do work that matters for people who care. No one is trapped in today's workplace. We get to choose.

You are doing something special for others and yourself by reading **Work Positive in a Negative World: Team Edition**! The investment of your time will come back multiplied with more confidence and enthusiasm and you'll discover your own Work Positive that will inspire and encourage others along the way.

Dan Miller, *New York Times* bestselling author
of *48 Days to the Work You Love* (www.48Days.com)

Why a Team Edition:

What I Learned Since 2011

> *"I've learned that people will forget what you said,*
> *people will forget what you did, but people will*
> *never forget how you made them feel."*
> —Maya Angelou

The first edition of *Work Positive in a Negative World* was published in 2011. The business environment was unfriendly, struggling to emerge from the long shadow of the Great Recession. Lay-offs, cut-backs, and closures dominated the daily news.

My company, like so many, was rocking along successfully until the fourth quarter of 2008. The economy's positive waves carried most of us to the shores of success.

Then it all changed in a moment.

Previous to the change, I traveled speaking and coaching. I recognized the change fully one day when my wife looked at me and said, "Honey, shouldn't you be traveling?"

The Great Recession had slaughtered the cash cow I rode.

And yet I knew intuitively that Dr. Norman Vincent Peale was right when he said, "Within every adversity lies the seeds of opportunity."

I buried the cash cow and started looking for seeds.

That's when I unearthed the five core practices of Great Depression gurus and planted them. The harvest was abundant and nourishing for my business as well as others with whom I shared the seeds of these five core practices. Top talent joined teams. Team members stayed longer. They created a positive work culture that increased productivity and profits.

I have continued to plant these seeds and reap a bountiful harvest since that book's publication. Then I hit a stone wall of reality in company after company regardless of industry. The first edition of this book was written for entrepreneurs and business owners. I was one and could speak to the rises and falls of doing business post-Great Recession. The tribe of Work Positive business owners who changed their attitudes and actions met with some success. While their Ripple Effect was demonstrable, their reach was short.

My mountain-sized discovery since 2011 is this: sure, CEOs and business owners lead with great influence over their work culture. And yet at the end of the workday, it's the middle managers, supervisors, and their teams that get the work done. They do the heavy lifting of moving the company or organization forward to achieve goals. They primarily create a Work Positive or a Work Negative culture.

Yes, vision-casting is Leadership 101 as is clarity around KPIs and everything else all of the HBR leadership studies prove. And yet the reality I discovered is that there is often a giant disconnect between executive leaders and their managers, supervisors, and teams. Business owners and CEOs can discover how to create a Work Positive culture and yet until they effectively interpret what that means for the rest of the company, it's business as usual. The negative world wins.

The truth is this: any organizational culture improvement that expects the C-suite to trickle down the desired new reality of a positive work culture dooms itself to damming up at middle management.

I've talked with thousands of middle managers, supervisors and their team members who are miserable at work. Read any survey and you find the results vary slightly and the outcomes are the same: between 67% and 75% of American workers surveyed rate themselves as either dissatisfied or very dissatisfied at work. That's at least two of three of your neighbors, and everyone else you know.

What happens at work rarely stays at work. The effects are stark and very real.

A driver cut off a fellow driver changing lanes on a 4-lane highway that runs through rural Virginia where I live. The cut-off driver sped up and forced the other guy off the road into a convenient store parking lot, jumped out and shot him. Dead.

Who does that without a dramatic source of misery daily?

Isolated event? Google "road rage" and see what you find.

And while you're there, search for "suicide." The rate is increasing dramatically among all demographics in an alarming trend. Teen suicides are rising quickly. A sixth-grade girl in our little rural community ended her life recently because of others teasing her daily as she went to the office for asthma medication. When I was in sixth grade my biggest worry was zits.

What 6th grader takes her own life except one living and working in a social fabric that's ripping and tearing daily?

The "opioid abuse" is often characterized as an epidemic. Read any research article findings. The misery is greater than our coping skills, so we anesthetize.

The one consistent experience all of us share is work. Work misery warps our social experiences and communities in a dramatically negative manner.

"Find another job," you say.

Since COVID, that's what millions of Americans did. The Great Recession that started this work transformation morphed into The Great Resignation. Over 47 million Americans voluntarily resigned in 2021. The trend continued into 2022 with over 4.5 million resigning in one month—March, 2022—alone.

Maybe you were one of those. How did that work out for you?

The lucky team members upgraded to a Work Positive culture in one of the client companies or organizations our company partners with.

The majority left one job, usually because of a negative boss, and found that the next one is just as bad.

The Great Resignation is morphing into The Great Regret. Job search site The Muse discovered that 72 percent of those who resigned experienced either surprise or regret that the new position or company they quit their job for turned out to be quite different from what they were led to believe. In fact, the *Guardian* reports that 48% of those workers want their old job back. A USA TODAY survey found that just 26% of job switchers like their new job enough to stay.

Members of The Great Resignation movement aren't the only ones with regrets. Companies are regretting some of their new hires as inflation rises and exerts new pressures to decrease expenses because of shrinking profits.

The beat goes on.

Why?

However well-intended the C-suite's positive work culture enhancements may be, the efforts dam up and work cultures remain negative unless managers and teams receive ownership of and responsibility for its co-creation.

We must empower everyone to create a Work Positive culture for the benefit of everyone.

But how do we do that?

It was 1989. I watched live TV news in horror as a lone Chinese man with a bandana covering his face stared down a tank in Tiananmen Square in Beijing. The devastation and death that followed was beyond reprehensible.

I watched as CNN anchor Bernard Shaw said something like: "The Chinese have two characters which they use to represent the word, 'crisis.' One means 'danger.' The other, 'opportunity.'"

How do we empower everyone to create a Work Positive culture for the benefit of everyone?

We risk the danger and seize the opportunity.

The risk is to challenge the status quo. Status quo literally means "what a mess we're in." The danger is that the mess is here to stay . . .

. . . unless we seize the opportunity.

Here's the opportunity: managers and teams can begin today to co-create a Work Positive culture rather than waiting for someone higher up to do it for them. In fact, managers and teams are uniquely positioned to Work Positive faster because their leverage is longer than the C-suites—do the math—and better because they face forward toward production and customers.

This *Team Edition* of *Work Positive in a Negative World* is for the managers and teams; the 67% to 75% who rate themselves as somewhere between dissatisfied and very dissatisfied at work and yet must spend 70% of their waking hours working just to pay the bills. It's for the middle managers and supervisors who know their team members by name and which one's marriage is falling apart from domestic abuse, who's addicted to pills or alcohol, whose kids are cutting themselves or acting out, and who's about to lose his truck because he lacks money management skills. This *Team Edition* is for all of the team people who get up and go to work daily and ask, "Is this it?"

There is more. A lot more.

You can Work Positive.

Yes, you can create a Work Positive culture that attracts top talent, reduces team turnover and increases productivity and profits.

Yes, you can Work Positive despite the disconnect, The Great Recession, The Great Resignation, The Great Regret and whatever next "The Great" is that tomorrow brings.

After all, you—the managers and teams—do the heavy lifting at work that drives every economy on the planet.

The one thing vital to understand and implement to reverse the current trends and uncontrollable external conditions is this: a positive work culture is the strong hand on the rudder that steers us all. We all sail together—C-suite, managers, and teams—or we all sink separately. Let's sail and steer together so that the wake we leave creates a rising tide of positivity that lifts ships for generations yet to come.

Yes, we can Work Positive.

This book is about how.

Along with this book, you get free bonuses. They are the:

- **Work Positive Checklist** – a simple checklist that coaches you to attract top talent and reduce team turnover.

- **Work Positive 5 Core Practices Cheat Sheet** – use this easy-to-follow guide to implement the 5 habit-sets of the Work Positive framework.
- **Work Positive Grab & Go Inspirations** – quick read positive thoughts to start your day in the best mindset.
- **Work Positive Affirmations** – begin each day the Work Positive way. Listen as Dr. Joey shares positive affirmations to focus on the positive and filter out the negative.

Also, you get a free membership in the Work Positive Community online. As you read this book, you discover coaching boxes, Consider How You Work Positive . . . " Each of these are your reading pitstops to apply what we just talked about. You can answer them in your mind or take notes. Or, join the Work Positive Community to learn more from others like yourself who want to create a positive work culture that increases productivity and profits. Each of the coaching box questions are topics in the Work Positive Community online. Your free membership allows you to answer the questions online, learn from others' answers, and comment on them. The Work Positive Community is a learning lab of ideas for how you create a positive work culture that attracts top talent and reduces team turnover.

Scan this QR code to set up your free account for both the book bonuses and the Work Positive Community.

You Can Work Positive

"A dream you dream alone is only a dream.
A dream you dream together is reality."
—John Lennon

How is it that you work in the same company with other people, and yet do it so differently?

How is it that some of us perceive our current reality and interpret it as the worst of economic times, no opportunities, nothing will work out right, negative?

And others of us perceive the current reality and interpret it as the best of economic times, overflowing with opportunities, everything will work out fine, positive?

What makes the difference?

Linda started her own business, which became successful financially, but at a great cost. She rarely took a complete weekend off, and never took a vacation. Her husband and two young children went on trips without her.

After five years, she decided to take a vacation and enjoy some extended time off, getting to know her husband again and enjoying her children. So, she called her three vice presidents in for a meeting, and told them, "As you know, we've all worked hard to grow this company. I've ensured through these five years of hard work that each of you had some time away. But I didn't do for myself what I did for you.

"So, the time has come for me to take an extended vacation. I'm taking the next year off to enjoy my family. The only way I can do this is for you to lead in my absence.

"While I'm gone, I expect each of you to carry on as if I were here. And as an added bonus, I've deposited money in your department's account. Jill, you'll find $50,000 to invest in the business as you see fit. John, you're receiving $20,000 to invest in the business as you deem appropriate. And Bob, you'll find $10,000 to invest using your talents to grow this business. I'll be back a year from now and expect an accounting at that time." And Linda got up from her desk and left. Jill, John, and Bob sat dumbfounded for a moment, and then stumbled over to the window overlooking the parking lot. "There she goes," Jill said. "She's really doing this."

"And for a whole year," John said. "Who would have thought it?"

Bob said, "Must be a trick or a test of some sort. She'd never leave us alone for that long with so much additional money."

Jill turned away from the window. "Well, you guys can stand here if you want to, but I've got $50,000 to invest in this business so I'm going to get busy." She walked out the door, down the hall, and toward her office.

"Yeah, me, too," said John, as he pulled his smartphone out to make a call, walking down the hall to his office.

"I still think it's a trick or something," Bob said, as he stood there in Linda's office.

A year passed more quickly than Linda imagined it would. She found herself back in her office, meeting with Jill, John, and Bob again. After chit-chatting about some of the highlights of her extended vacation, Linda said, "OK, Jill, tell me what you did with my $50,000 while I was gone."

Jill put a P&L up on the screen and said, "Linda, I invested it in marketing a new division within our company to an underserved target group. You'll see at the bottom of this sheet that I doubled your $50,000. There's $100,000 profit there."

"Great work, Jill! That's exactly what I hoped for. And because of your marvelous achievement, Jill, I'm making you a partner in the company. Here's a contract for you to read over and let me know what you think. Now John, it's your turn. What did you do with my $20,000 while I was on the beach relaxing?"

"You're gonna love this, Linda," John said as he put a Gantt chart on the screen. "When you left, I studied our inventory liquidity and discovered some items that hang around a little too long in our warehouses, clogging up our cash flow. So, I invested in new software and hardware for an updated inventory control system, negotiated with our vendors for tighter shipping, and well . . . you can see for yourself."

"Wow, John! You turned that department around to the tune of $40,000 by solving that problem. You're awesome, John! So, let me do something awesome for you," and she handed him a contract. "Read this over and let me know what you think about becoming a partner in the company. Bob, it's your turn. Tell me something good!"

"Well, Linda," Bob said hesitantly, "I know you have very high standards, and I know you hate carelessness. You demand the best and don't tolerate a lot of mistakes. I was afraid I would disappoint you, so I wrote a check for the $10,000 you left me and put it in the company safe. And here it is, safe and sound—your $10,000."

Linda's face turned red, then scarlet. "Bob," she said, "I've been gone a whole year, and the best thing you could do with $10,000 is to let it sit in the company safe?'

"Yes," Bob said. "It's all there."

"The least you could have done," Linda said while standing up, "was to have put it in a money market account somewhere. But you couldn't even do the least, could you, Bob? At least I would have gotten a little interest."

"I just thought it best to play it safe," Bob said.

"Play it safe?" Linda asked. She took a deep breath. Then she said, "You know, Bob, you're right. Play it safe. Great policy. I'm going to play it safe, too."

She handed the $10,000 check to Jill and said, "Jill, here's $10,000. Invest it as you think best."

Then turning to Bob, she said, "Bob, I'm going to play it safe some more. Go clean out your desk. You won't go out on a limb for me no matter how much fruit grows out there. So, I can't go out on one for you, either. Take your things and leave."

Jill, John, and Bob were each in the same situation and circumstances. They had the same empowered choices and opportunities.

Jill and John redefined their realities, and achieved their dreams. They are partners in the company.

Bob achieved nothing except getting fired.

How is it that you work in the same company with other people, and yet do it so differently?

I grew up hearing my grandparents talk about the Great Depression. The Great Depression is the best example of working in the same business environment and doing it so differently.

Dale Carnegie wrote *How to Win Friends and Influence People* in the middle of the Great Depression. The book promised imminent success and sold more copies than any other book except the Bible up to that point. His other books continue to sell strongly and his training seminars are taught internationally today.

How did Dale Carnegie create a company in the Great Depression that still thrives today? What did he do differently?

Also, during the Great Depression, a Kentucky grandfather started cooking chicken. People loved his chicken so much that despite going bankrupt, he took his chicken along with eleven secret herbs and spices on the road in his station wagon. I'll bet you've eaten chicken prepared "Colonel" Harland Sanders' way at a KFC (Kentucky Fried Chicken).

What did Colonel Sanders do during the Great Depression that made It the best of times for our fried chicken cravings today?

There were two young electrical engineering graduates who started an electrical machine business in a rented garage in Palo Alto, California, during the Great Depression. Bill Hewlett and Dave Packard officially became business partners in 1939. Most likely you have used a printer or computer with the "HP" label on it.

What propelled Bill and Dave out of the Great Depression doldrums into amazing technology success today?

For most people, the Great Depression was the worst of times. For Dale Carnegie, Colonel Sanders, Hewlett and Packard, and others like them, it was the best of times.

What did they know about how to work that you can learn and prosper from today?

You can create a positive work culture that attracts top talent, reduces team turnover, and increases productivity and profits just like Dale Carnegie, Colonel Sanders, Hewlett and Packard, and others. You can choose to work like Jill and John instead of Bob.

How?

You attract top talent, reduce team turnover and create a positive work culture that increases productivity and profits as you discover how to Work Positive.

The purpose of this book is to coach you to Work Positive like Jill and John.

If a 9-year-old boy can learn to do it, so can you.

Like most 9-year-old boys, this one wanted a new bicycle. He wanted a new three-speed bike in the worst sort of way. His parents told him he had a bike and to just be satisfied. Of course, he didn't listen, and tried to earn some summer money for the bike of his dreams the way most young boys do—mowing grass.

Only this little guy had allergies and asthma so extreme that his financial enterprise caused a viral infection in his lungs. He was hospitalized at the best pediatric allergy and asthma center in the world at that time, Duke University Hospital. One evening, the doctors told his mother, "We've done all we can."

His mother peered through the mist tent at the boy lying there in the hospital bed, looked deeply into his eyes, and said, "You can hold on through the night. I am positive that you can do this."

And he did. He recovered, came home, and, still determined to get a new bike, sold inscribed Christmas cards door-to-door in the heat of August. His neighbors bought his cards; a lot of cards. He asked the folks with whom his dad worked, "How many beautiful Christmas cards with your family's name inscribed inside would you like?" They bought a lot of cards, too. He asked the folks at his church with the same result. He asked everyone unable to resist his boyish smile. This 9-year-old boy who wanted a new three-speed bike sold so many inscribed Christmas cards that he bought his new bike . . . and a telescope . . . and a cassette recorder/ player--the latest technology.

Years later, the little boy grew up and was seventeen years old when his dad came home early from a business trip one day and explained that an international company had bought the business for which he worked. They had pulled all of the cash out of it and were shutting it down, eliminating his job. "I don't know how we'll pay for your college," he said. The dad cried for the very first time in front of the son.

The now-teenaged boy remembered selling Christmas cards. He knew he could pay his way through college. So, he drove to the local AM/FM radio station, and with no experience, walked into the owner's office and two hours later walked out with a job as a disc jockey. At first, he just worked weekends—the times no one else wanted to work. Within six months, he had the number-one rated afternoon drive show in the market.

He completed his bachelor's degree, paying for it as a Program Director at a radio station. Later he finished a master's degree and a doctorate degree—paying as he studied and worked.

He went on to lead small, medium, and large organizations in turn arounds. He discovered that Dr. Norman Vincent Peale was right: "Within every adversity lies the seeds of opportunity."

Then one day, the 9-year-old boy reached midlife and decided it was time to start his own company, coaching people to create a positive work culture, the same way Dale Carnegie, Colonel Sanders, Hewlett and Packard, and he had.

I am that nine-year-old boy.

I studied Work Positive leaders like these Great Depression gurus and work from their principles. This book represents what I learned from them intellectually and what I discovered experientially in my own work life.

The backdrop for your Work Positive efforts is an unhealthy dependance on the market's economic conditions to determine how much success you achieve. You allow external circumstances to blueprint your internal processes. You abdicate your birth right to achieve fulfillment through work to the naysayers of negativity who chronically find something to complain about.

Why? Perhaps to have someone to blame for the economy. Maybe to avoid responsibility for failing to try.

Or, it could be you really desire to create a positive work culture, and don't know how. You work overwhelmed by the weight of this negative world rather than ask and learn.

This world is negative and its insidious reach pervades everything.

Turn on the TV to a 24/7 news channels. Listen carefully to the news reporters' words. "If it bleeds, it leads" is the journalistic mantra. Or, check out your local TV station and watch local news. They import stories of murders, fires, and business closings from around the world if your neck of the woods lacks enough bad news of devastation, disaster, and doom that day.

Or, if you can find a newspaper, read the lead headline for a week. Track the content and how it is reported. Something is always rotten in Denmark. It's only news if the man bites the dog, not if the dog bites the man, and there's a whole lot of biting going on. If there's not, there ought to be, so let's publish an editorial predicting the end of the biting economy.

Or, listen to talk radio in the afternoon for a week. Sure, try out different personalities on different stations. You discover a great deal of commonality in style—attack and destroy the "other side," and promote your own. Chicken Little pundits say, "The sky is falling," and it is someone else's fault. "If the world would just do what I say, I could solve all the problems because I am the hero" fills the airwaves all afternoon. A tsunami of negative egocentricity floods our public airwaves.

Let's get more personal. Ask someone who is negative and dissatisfied at work, "How are you?" Then listen to the litany of problems, predicaments, and pathos.

The world is negative.

And you're trying to work in it.

So, how's that going for you?

You are a part of the problem when you participate in the world's negativity and allow it to define your reality. You join the herd mentality and graze from negative clump to negative clump, working because you have to.

That's why this book is so important right now. You attract top talent, reduce team turnover and create a positive work culture that increases productivity and profits when you choose to Work Positive in a negative world.

Sure, there are a ton of problems to tackle in the negative world. The list is long and exhausting.

And yet if you continue to bring the same mental models to these problems, you will get more of what you already have.

The purpose of this book is to coach you to create a Work Positive culture. To do what Dale Carnegie, Colonel Sanders, Hewlett and Packard and other Great Depression gurus did to Work Positive in the worst of economic conditions.

If they can do it, so can you.

What did they do that you can do?

They mentally focused on the positive and filtered out the negative. They replaced negative thoughts with positive ones. They Perceived the positive at work, the first core practice.

They focused on positive people and filtered out the negative relationships with those co-workers I call "Eeyore Vampires." They Conceived the positive at work, the second core practice.

They decided to emotionally redefine their work reality and fulfill their dreams. They engaged their work with purpose and passion and understood the negative world as filled with disguised opportunities. They Believed the positive at work, the third core practice.

Then they discovered that by paying attention to positive thoughts and positive people and stating their intentions of believing in the positive and by acting on their attention and intention, they could do what others saw as impossible. They Achieved the positive at work, the fourth core practice.

And as they created a positive work culture that increased productivity and profits, these Great Depression gurus said, "Thank you!" They served others. They discovered that like Jill and John, you reap what you sow. They Received the positive at work, the fifth core practice.

I refer to these as core practices because they are a combination of attitude that works from the core of who you are and practices which are actions aligned with your attitude that you do daily until they become habits. These five core practices—Perceive, Conceive, Believe, Achieve, and Receive—are the mind, relationships, heart, activity, and soul of your Work Positive work culture.

This book starts you on the path to Work Positive right where you are in your current workplace. You discover actions you can take today to Perceive, Conceive, Believe, Achieve, and Receive your Work Positive work culture. Your actions emerge from a new awareness you discover about work and how you best work. Your new awareness pops up from a positive attitude toward your work.

One of the most powerful actions you can take with this book is to spend some time thinking over the questions and items in the "Consider How You Work Positive. . ." boxes. Think of it as coaching in a box. These coaching boxes are the 20% of this book that'll make 80% of the positive improvement in your actions, awareness, and attitude.

Also, at the end of each chapter, you'll find a "Grab & Go" summary. These quick statements crystallize the major points of what you just read and are great for a quick pick-me-up when the negative world beats you down.

The first edition of this book helped so many executives and owners Work Positive. It was a best-seller numerous times in a variety of categories. Even business book clubs read it together along with their leadership teams.

Others read the first edition introspectively, considering deep within themselves how to Work Positive in a negative world and achieve their business dreams. Later they talked about it with others.

College students read chapters and engaged in deeper learning from one another in online communities.

However, you approach this book, you can enjoy a Work Positive work culture in this negative world. This book shows you how.

There are a couple of major differences between this Team Edition and the previous.

First, I have coached and spoken to hundreds of thousands of people about how to Work Positive in the years since the first edition came out. I have learned a great deal from them and hopefully returned the favor. This Team Edition reflects these real-time discoveries.

Second, the first edition was written primarily for business owners and entrepreneurs. As I told you in the preface, this Team Edition is written more for middle managers, supervisors, and their teams who want more from their work. I have found through the years that to create sustainable work like the Great Depression gurus, we must attract top talent and reduce team turnover, the first two benefits of the Work Positive work culture. And yet by far the most meaningful benefit of top talent attraction and reduced team turnover is that you create a positive work culture that increases productivity and profits. Your time and attention given to activities that fulfill you personally creates greater satisfaction. This positive legacy outlives you as you move from dissatisfied to satisfied because you make a life worth living. I think of it as eternal fun. And I am serious about having fun. Just ask the people who work with me . . .

Core Practice 1:

PERCEIVE the POSITIVE at Work

chapter 1

You Can Perceive the Positive at Work

"I am an old man and have known a great many troubles,
but most of them never happened."
—Mark Twain

I was lying flat on my back in the grassy outfield, trying to come to. I had drifted back from my third-base position for the Little League team White Sox into shallow left field to catch a fly ball. I missed the ball with my glove and instead caught it with my forehead.

I remember hearing, "Son, you've got to keep your eye on the ball."

About that same time, I walked into my fourth-grade classroom, sat down at my desk, and pulled out my notebook paper and pencil just as Mrs. Wheeler ordered. It was time for math, and she flipped on the overhead projector. More math problems, but for some reason, I couldn't make them out. Assuming that the then-new technology wasn't functioning correctly, I asked Mrs. Wheeler, "Would you please focus the problems on the screen? I can't see them."

"Well, you're sitting right under them. I don't know why you can't," she said. "Stop trying to get attention and just do your work, Joey."

Now fast-forward 30-something years. I'm sitting in my favorite recliner, trying to read a book and not doing so well.

"There's not enough light in this room," I told my wife. "And have you noticed how small they're making the print these days? Must be a cost-cutting move to save paper."

I played yo-yo with the book trying to get it the right distance for me to read, discovered I couldn't, and said, "My arms must have shrunk from all those hot showers during my teenaged years."

I caught two more fly balls with my forehead before they figured it out. I can still remember the first fly ball I squeezed into my glove, breathing a sigh of relief.

I saw my grades go from A's to C's before they figured it out. They went back up to A's afterwards.

I noticed that I was reading a lot less before I figured it out. I was like a kid again when I could read without difficulty.

What did we figure out?

I needed glasses in fourth grade and bifocals at midlife.

My perception was off.

Your mental perception of work gets blurry, too. How can you tell? What are the pop-flies you miss at work? Your grades going down? Quit reading?

Discovering how you mentally Perceive or think about your work is the first key to increasing sales with greater productivity so you get out of the office earlier to do what you love with those you love--your Work Positive work culture. Focusing on the positive and filtering out the negative at work until it becomes a habit requires you to separate what dominant thoughts play in your head from those you want to play.

For instance, you can assume the blurriness comes from working in a negative world. You can react and blame your economic problems on the negative world, much like I experienced with my vision.

"Son, keep your eye on the ball."

"Stop trying to get attention and just do your work, Joey."

"There's not enough light in this room."

There is always someone encouraging you to play the blame game. And it's easy to camp out there, join the majority chorus, and blame an economic downturn on the negative world. You settle for less than your work can be. You limit how you think about it.

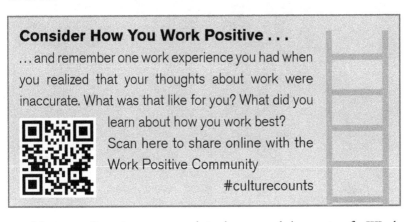

Consider How You Work Positive . . .

. . . and remember one work experience you had when you realized that your thoughts about work were inaccurate. What was that like for you? What did you learn about how you work best?

Scan here to share online with the Work Positive Community

#culturecounts

How you Perceive your work is the mental dynamic of a Work Positive work culture. You choose the thoughts you focus on as they relate to work, positive and negative. Let's look at how you Perceive your work, the obstacles to perceiving it positively, and how you can focus on the positive at work, filter out the negative, and help create a sustainable Work Positive environment.

chapter 2

Focus Your Thoughts

"I'm not sure what the future holds, but I do know that I'm going to be positive and not wake up feeling desperate. As my dad said, 'Nic, it is what it is, it's not what it should have been, not what it could have been, it is what it is.'"

—Nicole Kidman

I remember the first time I played the game where someone tells you not to think about something. You've played it before where someone mentions an object like an elephant in a pink tutu and tells you not to think about it. Of course, what's the first thing that flashes in your mind? That elephant in the pink tutu, right?

Your mind focuses your thoughts very quickly with only a little suggestion.

So why is it such a challenge for you to focus your thoughts on the positive dynamics of your work? Your mind requires coaching to filter out some thoughts and focus on others. Otherwise, it flashes to whatever shiny attention grabber presents itself--positive or negative. Your mind is like a muscle. You exercise it by conscious choice and strengthen it to think about the best instead of the worst of your work experiences.

Like a skilled surgeon, you identify the negative experiences and carefully remove them, creating room for the positive thoughts to flourish.

Mental Surgery is Necessary

My wife's lifelong dream was to live on a small farm and own some horses and board other people's. Our two daughters loved the idea as well . . . until it came time to plant the fence posts around the pastures. My two "employees" called in sick.

So, I phoned a friend or two who helped me plant fence posts. It was back-breaking labor, but it wasn't my back that hurt. It was my shoulder. The repetitive motions created scar tissue in my left shoulder joint that made my shoulder "freeze up."

The doctor and the therapist explained to me during the post-surgical physical therapy that the shoulder joint operates out of what is actually a system of supporting muscles in my upper chest and back. The joint is left to pull more of its weight than intended when these muscles weaken. My weak muscles left my shoulder joint vulnerable, which is why the scar tissue built up and the shoulder froze.

Your mind is like my shoulder. It requires strengthening. The other four core practices to Work Positive—Conceive, Believe, Achieve, and Receive—comprise that muscle group. A flabby, unfit mind simply chases whatever thought about your work enters it or whatever thought someone else suggests about it, positive or negative. Your mind freezes up; that is, mental scar tissue builds up in your mind, and you become susceptible to whatever thought shows up. Mental surgery then becomes necessary to remove the negative thought-scar tissue that makes you unattractive to top talent, teams run out of the back door, and productivity and profits decrease.

Your mind requires a strength and conditioning program. Let's take a look at how it works so you can begin your Perceive training program. You watch a report on a news channel that says the economy is contracting, that manufacturing is down, that consumer confidence is at its lowest point, and "top economists" predict a dramatic rise in inflation in the next quarter. Now, the company you work for has grown stronger for the last six consecutive quarters. The bottom line is firm. And yet what do you do when you work in purchasing and your best vendor calls to confirm your next quarter's order? You shrink the order despite your positive track record.

Or, let's say you're watching your favorite TV program, and a commercial comes on for a snack food. You weren't hungry before, but suddenly you are. The next thing you know, you're getting up and heading to the kitchen for snack food.

The power of suggestion is so strong. Your mind received the impression, activated a hunger impulse, and triggered your legs to move. You really didn't even think about it. It just happened.

Or, did it? What if you choose instead to focus your thoughts? What if you made the decision to cut out snacks between meals? Your mind is made up. You choose healthy over the commercial's suggestion. You think about getting a snack and decide against it. You hide the snack foods or, better yet, refuse to bring them home. It's more important to be healthy than to chase a snack commercial into the kitchen. Your mind was made up before the commercial ever appeared.

"But Dr. Joey," you say. "It's not that easy to focus my work thoughts on the positive."

Actually, it is. Here's how.

Your mind was made to focus. It focuses on something every minute of every day, even when you're sleeping.

Still unsure if you can do it?

As soon as you read the opening paragraph about the dancing elephant in the pink tutu, what did you see in your mind? The same one you see right now?

Your mind focuses on something every minute of every day and night. It is the way your brain functions. Instead of questioning if you can focus your mind, the better question is, "What do I choose to focus on?"

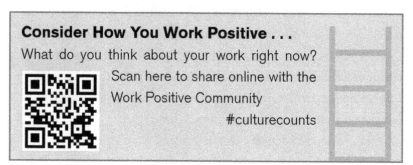

Consider How You Work Positive . . .

What do you think about your work right now?

Scan here to share online with the Work Positive Community

#culturecounts

You See What You Look For

Let's say you are interested in buying a new vehicle. You go to the dealer's car lot and look at a white Honda Accord. You even decide to test-drive it. You really like it. You can see yourself in it, but the salesperson just won't get the price right for you. You leave the lot to think about the purchase some more. As you turn out of the dealer's lot and drive down the street, guess what you see? A white Honda Accord. You think, "That's interesting."

You pull out onto the expressway and merge into traffic right behind . . . a white Honda Accord.

You look across the median at the traffic headed in the opposite direction. What kind of car passes you? That's right, a white Honda Accord.

You think to yourself, "There are white Honda Accords everywhere!"

Think again.

Your mind focused on the white Honda Accord you just drove.

You saw what you chose to see.

You see what you look for.

You focus your mind every minute of every day and night on something. What do you choose to focus on?

Where is your work focus—on the positive or the negative?

The world has plenty of negative mental energy for you to Perceive. Denial of negativity in the work world is fruitless at best and stupid at worst. It is ridiculous to expect your work culture simply to overwhelm you with positivity. Your boss or team leader, your customers or clients, your co-workers, your _____ (insert the rest of them here) will not get you out of bed and stand in line to fill your mind with positive thoughts about your work every morning. Your mind is yours to focus. The Work Positive culture you want is yours because you choose it.

What will you choose to Perceive?

You see what you look for.

Vultures fly over the desert, looking for dead animals. They search for fallen carcasses to consume.

Hummingbirds fly over the same desert, looking for something different. Hummingbirds look for flowers growing from a cactus or near a pond. They search for floral displays to eat from.

The difference between the vulture and the hummingbird is what they look for. They fly over the same desert. The vultures see death to feast on because that's what they look for. The hummingbird looks for life-giving flowers.

You look for what you choose to see as you fly over work and the culture that surrounds it—failures or successes, losses or leverage; the negative or the positive.

Then you consume what you see. Your choices determine how successful you are. Your choices establish whether or not you attract top talent, reduce team turnover and create a positive work culture that increases productivity and profits.

You see what you look for.

My wife and I ate together in a restaurant when the owner approached us. We're friends in addition to being patrons so I stood and hugged her. She put her hands around my waist, patted it, and said, "Have you lost weight?"

"No," I said, "must be this floppy shirt."

"Well, I definitely think you've lost weight," she said.

I stood back for a moment and noticed her waistline. She had lost weight, and a lot of it.

"You're the one who's lost weight," I said. "Well, yes, I have," she replied.

A few minutes later as we continued our meal, another friend came over to say hello. I stood and hugged her. This woman also hugged my waist, patted my sides, and said, "Have you gained weight?"

"No," I replied, "must be this floppy shirt."

"Well," she said, "I definitely think you've gained some weight."

I stood back for a moment and noticed that she had gained weight. A lot of it. Fortunately, I had the good sense not to comment this time.

I sat back down, and my wife started laughing and I did, too, and said, "So, which is it? Have I lost or gained weight?"

"I wouldn't wear that floppy shirt anymore if I were you," she said.

So, who did we learn more about in these two conversations— me or these two women?

We see what we look for.

What do you see when you look at your work?

Show Me What You Can Do

When our daughters were much younger, I chose to spend as much time as I could with them. We did things like hike up a mountain or fish in a pond or plant flowers. When faced with a challenge during our adventures, they would say, "Daddy, I can't do it."

My response was always the same: "Don't tell me what you can't do. Show me what you can."

As they grew older and life became more complicated in middle and high school, they said, "Daddy, I can't do it." And I replied, "Don't tell me what you can't do. Show me what you can."

Then they started adulting with careers and marriage and children and said, "Daddy, I can't do it." And I said . . . yea, you guessed it.

I'm sure at my funeral, one of them will talk about one of Daddy's favorite sayings was, "Don't tell me what you can't do. Show me what you can."

It is so easy to occupy your mind with what you can't do. It's a never-ending list. Since your mind focuses on something, anything, all the time, it will go to that never-ending list, especially in times of frustration and failure.

Focusing your mind on what you can do empowers your mental choice to Perceive the positive at work. Finding something you can do, doing it, and focusing on that success creates a positive thought in your mind which spreads quickly. That positive perception then becomes the jet fuel that releases your imagination to work on the rest of the learning experiences necessary to get the task done.

Your imagination soars to new heights of achievement at work with that high-octane fuel. You exercise the positive muscle group of your mind, focus on creating that Work Positive culture that increases productivity and profits, and pretty soon that which seemed impossible is possible, and you say to yourself, "I can see my work this way all the time!"

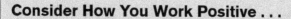

Consider How You Work Positive . . .

. . . and recall the last occasion when you were thinking about work and said, "I can't do it." What circumstances surrounded you in that moment? What prompted you to say that? What did you do after you said it? Scan here to share online with the Work Positive Community

#culturecounts

The Perception You Change May Be Your Own

My associate and I worked on a task together. She was in her office, I was in mine. She called to me from her office and said, "Look out your window and tell me what you see." So, I turned away from my desk, stared out the window, and said, "All I see is a house that needs to be torn down."

"No, look again," she said.

"I don't need to. Seriously, it's beyond repair," I said.

She walked into my office, raised the blinds, pointed and said, "Not the house. What else do you see?"

Almost as if for the very first time, I saw them—beautiful, lilac- colored, in full bloom, azaleas that stood several feet high in front of the house.

"Aren't they beautiful?" she said.

And I said, "Yes, if you choose to see them."

It is so easy for your mind to focus on the negative at work just like mine did with the house, or vultures trolling for death. Instead, you can choose to focus your mental energy on perceiving the positive at work like azaleas, or hummingbirds sniffing out flowers. It's a conscious choice. Your mind focuses on something related to work all the time. It's just a matter of how you guide your thoughts to perceive the positive, choosing the best work qualities, not the worst; things to praise your teammates about, not things to curse them for; the beautiful way in which customers buy your products or use your services, not the ugly few who demand a refund.

Our younger daughter helped me discover how to focus on the positive at work when she was about 4 years old. We really enjoy feeding the birds in winter. We set up bird feeders in our yards almost every winter. The problem is that squirrels love bird seed, also.

So, I waged war on the bird-seed-stealing squirrels one winter. I borrowed an air rifle, and started looking for the "mangy tree rats." I looked for the squirrels every time I walked by our bay window, just waiting for them to show themselves so that I could grab the rifle, sneak outside around the corner of our home, and shoot them. I even put our younger daughter on alert—"Sweetie, let me know if you see a squirrel on our bird feeder."

That is, until one day she looked up at me and said, "Daddy, we used to look out the window for pretty birds. Now we look for ugly squirrels."

When she said that, I realized that all the joy of my bird feeder was gone. I wasn't looking for pretty birds and their magnificent colors anymore, but ugly, drab squirrels that I could shoot.

It's easy to see only the ugly, drab squirrels that invade your workplace. Those bushy-tailed thieves will steal your work focus if you let them. It's easy to stop looking for the beautiful qualities about work like the cha-ching of the cash register, or the relieved look on a customer's face when you solve a problem, or your relationships with teammates and clients.

I put down my weapon. I stopped looking for the ugly. I looked for the beautiful and I found it. Because I looked for it.

You see what you choose to see.

Consider How You Work Positive. . .

Think about an experience when you chose to see the ugly at work instead of something beautiful. Consider experiences like a hallway conversation in which you could have said something positive about a person or situation, but instead chose to say something negative. What could you have said or done differently? Scan here to share online with the Work Positive Community

#culturecounts

Your Mind Constantly Perceives

I sat, relaxing with a newspaper, enjoying some quiet time early one morning before the demands of my day started. All of a sudden, a bird began making all kinds of noises just outside the window. At first, I ignored it, but it continued and more loudly. So, I got up to investigate.

As I stepped out on the porch, I saw the baby mockingbird perched in a Japanese maple, squawking at Maybelle, our cat, who sat on the porch, staring off across the horse pasture. The bird who bothered me didn't seem to bother Maybelle at all.

Maybelle saw me on the porch and sauntered over, rubbing herself against my legs, letting me know that I had permission to pet her, which I did for a couple of minutes while she purred. All the while, this baby bird was still screaming at us, and Maybelle didn't mind. She focused on my petting instead of the noisy bird. She knew the bird was there and chose to ignore it.

There is always someone squawking at work, challenging your Work Positive work culture. They want your best team members to leave and make it hard to attract new ones. Someone like a squawking teammate complaining about the cheap coffee the company provides. Or, a squawking boss who thinks you're a Superperson and can leap tall problems in a single bound. Or, a squawking customer who's convinced you overcharged her a nickel.

As if work didn't provide you with enough squawking, you go home and the laundry has yet to put itself in the washing machine and the vacuum cleaner is still in the closet and the pot roast isn't in the Instapot and it's supper time and like hungry little birds, your partner or kids are squawking, "We're hungry. What's for supper?"

How do you focus on the positive at such times?

Consider How You Work Positive . . .

What can you learn from Maybelle about how to deal with the squawkers at work? How will you deal with them today? Scan here to share online with the Work Positive Community

#culturecounts

Imagination—Your Mental Jet Fuel

Maybelle can teach you a great deal about how to perceive the positive at work--focus your thoughts on the positive and filter out the negative. She chose to ignore the baby mockingbird. She filtered out the squawking and focused on the pastures, basking in the warm sunlight. She did more than just turn away from the negative. She turned toward the positive.

You have to do more than turn your mind away from the ugly squawkers to grow a Work Positive culture. You make a conscious choice to perceive the positive around you, focusing your mind on the best practices you can put into place, the things about your work worth praising, and the beautiful relationships you enjoy at work.

You create a mental vacuum when you choose to only ignore the negative aspects of work. Remember—your mind constantly focuses, whether you're awake or asleep. Your mind searches and discovers a thought or thing to fill itself with regardless of your intentions.

Your imagination is the jet fuel that powers your mental focus. It's equally good at perceiving the positive AND the negative at work and doesn't care which it does. It follows the trail you guide it down, consciously or subconsciously. Removing the negative thoughts about work from your mind is just part of the equation. Your imagination fills your mental void with worry.

Worrying about work focuses you on negative potential outcomes that may or may not become reality. Your mind fills itself with something, anything, even if that something only exists in your imagination.

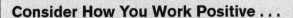

Consider How You Work Positive . . .

What were you worried about at work last year? How hard is it to remember? Scan here to share online with the Work Positive Community

#culturecounts

Perceive Through the Fog

Let's say that you understand how your imagination works and choose to focus on the positive, ignoring the negative aspects of work as much as possible. Your imagination starts asking for more information which you lack. Do you allow your thoughts to follow the rabbit of your imagination down that hole with questions like…

"What if my boss gets frustrated with me for something beyond my control?"

"What if a key teammate quits to start her own business?"

"What if my spouse says I'm never home and leaves me for someone else because I have to do three people's jobs?"

What happens in your brain when you descend into this imaginary negative work hole?

A mental fog rolls in. Worry slips in since you're unable to predict the future.

The kitchen in our home has a bay window that looks down the hill and across the horse pastures. It's really quite a beautiful sight . . . except when the fog rolls in. When the fog rolls in, we lose sight of the hill and pastures. We can't see the horses and insure they're safe. That's when our imaginations start asking for more information than we can supply and it's easy for us to worry.

Our minds rifle through 5,392 bad things that could happen to the horses, each one worse than another: a snake could bite one on the nose, one could step in a hole and hurt itself, one could get sick and die because we didn't call the vet in time, and the list goes on and on.

Nothing like this has ever happened to us.

And yet we still choose to worry since we are unable to predict the future.

You're that way, also. You worry about what is beyond your ability to see, like the "What if . . ." future of your work.

How many of the things you worry about actually happen?

Your inability to predict the future frustrates your brain's need for more information and negative thoughts pop up.

What do you do about it?

Mow Your Negative Mental Broom Straw

One thing you can do is to mow your negative mental broom straw.

I got on my tractor on a beautiful winter day and mowed a portion of our horse pasture. Broom straw grows over the winter. Occasionally the soil nutrients are a little off of what's best for growing grass and broom straw jumps up over the winter. It competes with the spring grass for nutrients, water, and sunlight. Horses eat grass and pick around the broom straw. So, I mow the broom straw.

Negative thinking is like broom straw. It competes for nutrients in your brain. Ever notice how one negative thought breeds another? And another? And pretty soon, there's an entire field of negative mental broom straw growing in your mind? You can choose to mow down your negative thoughts and in their place plant positive thoughts. Here are a couple of ways to do that.

First, seed each day well.

Each morning, I get up early to read and meditate. I plant positive thoughts in my mind. I sit in the kitchen. There are windows beside the bay window and on a nice morning, I'll raise them.

One morning, I sat sipping my coffee, rocking and meditating on the day ahead, eyes closed. I realized that the window was shut so I got up and raised it.

I heard a bird singing the most beautiful song as I raised it. I enjoyed its morning serenade announcing, "I made it through the night!" Then I thought, "I'm sure this bird was singing before I opened the window."

The work world today is a lot like that. There is so much positivity to Perceive, and yet you miss the music if the window to your mind is shut.

Choose to invest time every morning to throw open the window to your mind. Focus your mind on positive thoughts. Visualize positive activities. See positive achievements.

Avoid all "push media" such as TV and radio in the mornings. Why allow those who monetize negativity to choose your thoughts for you? Stay informed by "pull media" such as internet news sites where you can scan headlines and pull the stories you choose to read and watch. This positive, proactive approach guarantees you focus on your positive choices rather than abdicating your choice to network executives. The direct, positive impact on your work is you grow mentally more positive, which propels you to success.

Second, cultivate the day well.

Every night, get in bed before you want to go to sleep. Relax and write down or type about three positive experiences you're thankful for from that day. Call the book you write in or file you type in "The Gratitude Diary." You plant in your mind an attitude of gratitude that cultivates in your sleep overnight as your subconscious mind processes the day's experiences.

Be as specific as possible. Instead of saying, "I'm thankful for all the customers we had today," say, "I'm thankful for Sally who brought three of her friends to shop with us today." Or, instead of just saying, "I'm grateful for all my teammates today," say, "I'm grateful for Jonathan, who after our coaching session today, emailed me what he already did to move forward."

Being specific helps. You will feel more refreshed than usual the next morning because you cultivated these positive thoughts of gratitude in your mind and your brain processed them overnight. Remember: Your mind is knit together in such a way that your thoughts focus on what you choose day and night.

Consider How You Work Positive . . .

What do you currently do that feeds your mind positive thoughts daily? When will you try these two suggestions to seed and cultivate each day well? Scan here to share online with the Work Positive Community

#culturecounts

Focus on the Good Soil

One of the things I enjoy doing around our farm is planting grass seed in the horse pastures. One fall, I bought some sacks of good seed and loaded them in the spreader on the back of my tractor. I scattered the seed everywhere I could.

I noticed in the days following that the horses beat down a path through the pasture. They walk that same path every day so it's a hardened path where no grass grows. The birds came and ate the grass seed off of the beat-down path.

Some of the seed I scattered wound up in a pile of rocks stacked up around an oak tree. It grew pretty quickly and I could see the new green sprouts, but that's about as big as it ever grew. The roots were shallow, and the hot spring sun scorched it.

Some of the seed I scattered went outside of the fence line and over into a really thick area where blackberry bushes grow. The grass took root and shot up for a little while, but it just couldn't compete for sunlight and nutrients with the taller, more mature blackberry bushes. So, it died.

The rest of the seed I scattered fell on parts of the pasture that were good soil. They grew up in the spring, took solid root, and just kept growing. Soon I turned the horses back into that pasture and they loved all that new grass.

Where do you plant mental seeds of positivity?

You might say, "I just don't get it, all this talk about how my mind constantly focuses." You worked negative so long that you are the path my horses beat down—hard—so the good seed can't penetrate your mind.

You might say, "Yeah, I love it!" and start focusing your thoughts so you can enjoy a Work Positive culture, achieve a little success, and say, "I got it" and quit. Your experience will be like the grass that grew in the rock pile. You will wilt and die when the heat of change overwhelms you.

You may say, "I will turn my thoughts away from the negative," and miss filling your mind with positive thoughts. Worry rolls into your imagination like fog. The weeds of anxiety choke your imagination. Those weeds crowd top talent attraction and force your teams to leave.

Or, you can say, "This is the good stuff. I chose to focus my thoughts on the positive aspects of my work, and I want more." You, my friend, are ready for a beautiful growing experience that will feed you forever. Keep reading . . .

Consider How You Work Positive . . .

Be surgically honest and ask yourself: Which of the four responses listed above am I experiencing right now at work? Which one do I want to have? Scan here to share online with the Work Positive Community

#culturecounts

Grab & Go

As you "Focus Your Thoughts," remember:

1. The perception you change may be your own as you learn to Work Positive.
2. You see what you're looking for at work:
   a. A white Honda Accord
   b. Carcasses or cacti
   c. A dilapidated house or stunning azaleas
   d. Ugly squirrels or beautiful birds
   e. Squawking birds or more satisfaction
   f. Lost or gained weight
   g. "Don't tell me what you can't do. Show me what you can."
3. Worry fogs your perception about work.
4. Mow the mental broom straw about work out of your thoughts.
5. Raise the window of your Work Positive culture and listen as your work sings.
6. Focus your thoughts on becoming the positive soil of your company.
7. The seed of your work is good.

chapter 3

Avoid Only Familiar Thoughts

*"As a single footstep will not make a path on the earth,
so a single thought will not make a pathway in the mind.
To make a deep physical path, we walk again and again.
To make a deep mental path, we must think over and
over the kind of thoughts we wish to dominate our lives."*
—Henry David Thoreau

Several generations ago, a country doctor, who was an avid fox hunter, often took his dogs along to chase foxes while he waited for women to deliver their babies. There was also a barber in the area whose shop was a favorite place for telling stories. The barber listened to the doctor tell his stories, had never been fox hunting, and so persuaded the doctor to take him.

The two went up a mountain highway and turned the dogs loose. Soon the chase began at a furious pace. The gentlemen sat in the front seat of the truck, and occasionally the doctor would nudge the barber and say, "Just listen to that music." The barber listened carefully and said nothing.

This same routine happened every few minutes until finally the barber said, "Doc, I've listened closely for several minutes now, and I can't hear the music because your dogs keep barking."

One person's music is another person's dogs barking.

The familiar can obstruct the Work Positive culture you chase.

Super-Efficient or Basically Lazy?

Your brain functions affect how you perceive your work. The doctor and the barber heard the dogs differently. The doctor heard the dogs barking as music. The barber listened for another type of music, one more familiar to him.

Your brain loves the familiar. Here's what happens as you perceive your work:

1. A thought about work enters your mind.
2. Your brain sorts the information.
3. Your brain searches for a catalog in which similar information was stored previously. Your mind wants to place this new information in a folder labeled "Familiar." Your brain wants to file it there if it resembles something you've stored before.
4. Your brain tries to delete the thought, or put it in the "Recycle Bin" if the thought refuses to fit in a current category because it's unfamiliar.
5. It is at this moment that you say something like, "I don't understand" or "I've never done it this way before" or "I can't hear the music because your dogs keep barking." You label the unfamiliar thought as "Negative," and toss it.

Your brain has neural pathways that your thoughts ride on. These neural pathways are like interstate highways. Familiar thoughts traffic up and down them like sports cars on the Autobahn. Unfamiliar thoughts are like mopeds trying to run the Autobahn. Your brain loves the familiar thoughts and screams at the unfamiliar ones, "Either move over or get off the interstate."

The work world changes daily and confronts your mind with the unfamiliar. How do you deal with so much change?

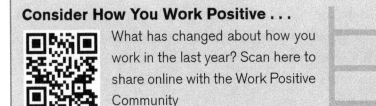

Consider How You Work Positive . . .

What has changed about how you work in the last year? Scan here to share online with the Work Positive Community

#culturecounts

Repeat After Me: "Repetition, Repetition, Repetition . . ."

Change at work assaults your mind with the unfamiliar daily. Change is thought of as negative because your brain prefers the familiar. The constant mental assault of change is exhausting which can make negativity your dominant thought.

And yet you have experienced constant change at work before.

Your work in third grade was to memorize multiplication tables. Do you remember when your teacher showed you all those multiplication tables and said you had to memorize them? What was your reaction?

"No way. No how."

And yet you found a way how and learned them. You carved out some new neural pathways in your brain. You created a new folder named "Times Tables."

How did you do it? Repetition.

Someone made you sit down and stare at them, saying them over and over until you got every single one of them correct. "Now was that so hard?" they asked you.

"Yes," you said. You knew even as a third grader how hard it is to create something new in a brain that loves the familiar.

You discovered that it requires a great deal of effort to hack your neural way through the jungle of the familiar to plant something unfamiliar.

Your brain is still super-efficient or lazy. It begs for the familiar and really tries to exclude anything that is uncharted territory. Your mind's primary function is survival, i.e., to keep you alive. It does not want you to march off the map of previous experiences because that's where danger lurks. It's where the wild things of work lurk.

Consider How You Work Positive . . .

Recall a recent experience in which you learned something new like how to operate a new piece of equipment, run some new software, or coach someone. How often did you say, "I don't know how to do this!" or "I've never done this before?" Scan here to share online with the Work Positive Community #culturecounts

So, here you are, reading a book titled *Work Positive in a Negative World: Team Edition*, hoping to figure out a way of creating more work positivity. Maybe you work negative. Negativity is familiar since you work in a negative world. Yes, it's miserable, and yet you choose it because it's familiar.

You want to Work Positive. You desire different, more positive results at work. You're praying that there is more to work than what you're experiencing. You realize to work in a different way, you must move beyond the same old behaviors . . . or else you'll go insane.

Your brain only longs for the familiar regardless of whether work is negative or positive.

Your mind interprets negative thoughts about work as familiar. It knows where to file them. It quickly sorts and processes them, pats itself on the back, and says, "What a good brain I am!" Your mind loves the familiar, even if it is negative.

So, how do you overcome its love of the negative familiar? Repetition.

That's right, you repeatedly, over and over, choose to Perceive the positive about your work and focus your mind on the unfamiliar success stories. You create some novel neural pathways that over time become familiar just like you did with your multiplication tables.

Who Moved My Coffeemaker?

My wife enjoys rearranging the kitchen counter periodically. She likes to play "spin the kitchen," so she shuffles everything around. The coffeemakers are moved from one side to the other, which means the canisters with the sugar and flour and stuff are moved to the other side of the stove.

I make the coffee every evening, programming our his-and-hers brewers to go off the next morning. The first evening I walk in to discover this new arrangement, I naturally go to the previous and familiar location of the coffeemakers and they're gone. So, I hunt around the kitchen, find it and begin my preparations, grumbling all the while. The unfamiliar is negative, right?

And of course, the coffee filters, which I had in a drawer near the previous location of the brewers, need relocating to a closer drawer. Then there's there are the coffees themselves, which previously was stored in a cabinet closest to the "familiar" spot. So, the coffees' location is changed as well.

That's a great deal of change to wake up with fresh coffee! Each time my wife spins the kitchen, it takes me about twenty-one evenings to stop walking over to the spot where I made coffee previously and reaching for filters and coffees that are no longer there.

The ways you work constantly change and move your coffeemakers. A new piece of diagnostic equipment is required to do repairs. A more efficient system is introduced into your franchise. A new safety rule is enforced by OSHA. You return to the same spot. Why? It's familiar.

Only through repetition—preparing the coffee every evening for twenty-one evenings in a row—do you unlearn the familiar and learn the new. That's right—unlearn the familiar and learn the new. It's a two-stage process. You do more than turn away from the negative aspects of work. You re-focus your thoughts on the positive. It's more than the old dog learning new tricks. We old dogs first unlearn the old tricks, clearing room in the brain for the new trick.

How long did it take me to stop moving to the previous location of the coffeemakers? About 21 days.

Sure, I got it right before then. I would get it right three evenings in a row, sometimes four, and then relax. That's when without even thinking about it I stepped over to the coffeemakers' previous location. It wasn't until after about twenty-one evenings that I could do it right unconsciously.

How did I finally stop that familiar behavior and act differently? Repetition.

Easier Said Than Done

Think of your mind's focus like a camera. Your smartphone has a camera with different lens functions like panoramic/landscape, normal, and zoom. Odds are you use only one or two functions on it. You have your "standard operating procedure" for taking pictures, which means your camera can do more tricks than you have yet to try. Why? You've never done photography this way before.

Our younger daughter received a new phone for Christmas one year. It had a far more powerful zoom than any of our others. I stood in our kitchen one evening as she sat across the room. Suddenly, she said, "Daddy, you need to trim your nose hairs."

She had zoomed up and in on my nose with the camera on her phone from her sitting angle. The status of my nose hairs was of great concern lest I go out in public and embarrass her in front of her teenaged friends.

Her powerful zoom was great for judging the status of my nose hairs, but when closed in so tightly, prevented her from seeing my eyebrows, eyelashes, and other facial features that I'm sure would have been equally offensive. She would have seen all of me, her mom, the kitchen counter, refrigerator and the rest of the appliances had she used the landscape/ panoramic lens. The zoom was myopic with a closed field of vision.

Your mind is set on a default zoom that myopically sees the familiar first. Your thoughts zoom in on it. The familiar ways worked for you in the past and quite well, so why change your field of vision now?

Or, have they? New challenges assault you each workday. Initially you judge them negatively because they are unfamiliar. They fail to fit your preconceived notions of how to do some task. You lack categories in which to insert them in your brain.

Consider How You Work Positive . . .

. . . and consider your typical reaction to a new marketing concept shared in a team meeting at work, or an unfamiliar shortcut that a friend offers to a client's office, or when the break room coffeemakers are moved. What's your reaction? Or, consider when the way to enter the building, or who can go to lunch when changes. What's the reaction? Scan here to share online with the Work Positive Community

#culturecounts

You resist the change only to wake up the next morning and discover that yesterday's change is joined by today's change, and tomorrow's change lurks in the shadows, ready to pop out when the clock strikes midnight.

The mantra "I've never done it this way before" is absolutely true. Redefining your reality from resistance to change to "That's right, and I'd better learn how to do it this way as quickly as possible to Work Positive" is critical.

So, What Is Your Typical Reaction to Something Unfamiliar?

Be honest, and remember: Your mind perceives the familiar first, even if it is negative.

You avoid thinking familiar, negative thoughts only through repetitive reprogramming of your mind to search out the positive aspects of work, zoom in on them, and hold your focus until your brain creates a new file folder.

You choose to Perceive work this way because you understand there are consequences if you remain stuck in the familiar. Those consequences, while unintended, move you further away from creating a Work Positive culture.

Our family enjoyed an extended weekend at the beach, just to relax and be together. I noticed a sandpiper one day as I sat with my wife and daughters, reading a book and relishing in the ocean. He was by himself, and soon I discovered why.

I watched him scurrying around the beach like most of his type looking for something to eat. At least that's what I thought he was doing. Soon I discovered that he used most of his time and energy to chase away other birds. If another sandpiper approached his territory, he quickly ran over to shoo him off. Then another bird invaded the opposite end of his area and he was off to chase her away. Back and forth that little bird ran, spending virtually no time eating and all his energy chasing away the competition.

How much of your daily mental energy do you waste defending your familiar turf at work, chasing away change like this paranoid sandpiper?

Before the old dog can learn new tricks, he must unlearn the old ones, creating room in his mind for the unfamiliar. So must the sandpiper. And so must you and I.

There is a cumulative effect on your work when you lock yourself up mentally in the familiar. Look around at the abandoned buildings that once housed businesses in your region. They're locked now, but the mental lock-up by that company took place long before the real estate was. Thinking only familiar thoughts is the sure path to poor results.

Your past success is no guarantee of future performance. Work changes daily. The work environment today slips in and away, ebbs and flows; no two days are exactly alike, despite what your brain tells you.

That's why it is imperative for you to avoid focusing only on familiar thoughts and create new neural pathways and categories in your mind. You search for the positive at work, learn positive practices from similar and dissimilar industries and adapt them, despite the unfamiliarity, and align your actions.

How do you avoid perceiving just familiar thoughts, which are often negative, and welcome unfamiliar ones?

Embracing the Unfamiliar

You force your brain through repetition to form new categories and file the positive until it becomes familiar. You implement this newly familiar positive and watch as your work grows. Top talent joins the team. Current talent stays. You create a positive work culture that increases productivity and profits. You Work Positive.

Soon you only want to focus on the positive at work. The positive at work becomes familiar and replace the negative thoughts.

My wife received some new horses to board from a farm about 2,000 miles away. The previous farm was set up differently than ours with the horses in a much smaller area. In fact, these four horses daily walked a 100-foot by 100-foot space.

So, when my wife put these horses into a five-acre pasture, you would think that the first thing they would do is to run all over it, happy to be in a significantly larger space, right?

Not so much.

At first, the leader of the herd stood basically in one spot all day. He was still enclosed in a very small space in his mind even though he had all five acres to enjoy. He refused to move.

When he did move a few days later, he walked a perimeter that measured 100-feet by 100-feet. He was a mental prisoner of the small space. He could not escape his familiar patterns even though he was unhappy, even miserable to the point of biting the other horses while in that small space.

The interesting thing for me was to watch him gently begin to explore our larger pasture. Gradually his mental picture of where he could graze expanded to include all the new, unfamiliar five-acre pasture. Repeatedly, he walked the previous space. Then he expanded his space bit by bit to include part of the unfamiliar pasture. Through repetition, he became more and more comfortable with more acreage.

After about twenty-one days of this tentative exploration, he burst into a gallop and surged through the pasture with reckless abandon, kicking up his heels, toward the fence line at the far end of the five acres. When he arrived at the fence, he just stood there for a moment, admiring the view. Then he turned to look back at where he had been, nickered to the other three horses, and they galloped to where he stood.

Your brain and the horse brain are similar: Your mind perceives the familiar first even if it is negative.

You avoid thinking familiar, negative thoughts only through repetitive reprogramming of your mind.

If a horse can do it, so can you.

Consider How You Work Positive . . .

. . . and relive an experience in which you faced a change at work and through repetition successfully navigated it. Put yourself back into the struggle of the change, and also revel in the sense of achievement and elation as you positively emerged on the other side. Remember the additional revenue generated. Recall your customers' faces as you provided a new solution to their problems. Relive your teammates' looks as "your change" worked. What was that like? Scan here to share online with the Work Positive Community

#culturecounts

Who Moved My Furniture?

I painted our master bedroom and my wife decided it was a great time to rearrange the furniture in the room. (See the pattern?) I like change . . . until I got up in the middle of the first night it was rearranged and bumped into a chair that wasn't there before. I almost didn't make it to the bathroom.

Then the second night I stubbed my little toe on a dresser. I sat down in the floor just to make sure it was still attached.

The third night I tried to knock off the little toe on the other foot on our bed. I was protecting the previously injured little toe. This time, I was down on my hands and knees, crawling around the bedroom, searching for my toe which I knew I had knocked off; praying it could be surgically reattached.

On the fourth night, I decided that perhaps I would do well to wake up and look where I was going. I didn't want to turn on a light and wake my wife. So, I started peering into the darkness more . . .

. . . and discovered that the dark really isn't so dark. The area light in a nearby horse pasture streams in through a window and lights part of my path. Later I discovered that on a night when there's a full moon, one portion of the room is bathed in light.

Sometimes your work life seems dark because you perceived only the negative familiar and that's led to injuries. You discover there is more light at work than you imagined; that you can peer into the dark shadows and find just enough unfamiliar positivity for your work journey to travel safely through the treacherous waters of daily change.

When you make this discovery of an unfamiliar, positive thought, repeat it.

Do it again. And again. And again.

Avoid only familiar thoughts. Perceive unfamiliar thoughts.

Then celebrate, because you've just taken another step to Work Positive, discovering how you focus on the positive and filter out the negative in the work world.

Grab & Go

Create a new mental file folder for these unfamiliar thoughts as you "Avoid Only Familiar Thoughts":

1. One person's music is another person's dogs barking.
2. Familiar thoughts are sport cars on the Autobahn. Unfamiliar thoughts are mopeds on the Autobahn.
3. Welcome unfamiliar thoughts with repetition. Welcome unfamiliar thoughts with repetition. Welcome unfamiliar thoughts with repetition.
4. Work constantly changes and moves your coffeemakers and furniture.
5. Your mind is set on a default zoom of what's familiar about work even if it's miserable.
6. Before the old dog can learn new tricks, he must unlearn the old ones.
7. How big is your work pasture . . . really?

chapter 4

Filter Your Thoughts

"You must not under any pretense allow your mind to dwell on any thought that is not positive, constructive, optimistic, kind."
—Emmet Fox

L et me be completely honest with you. I work for my wife on our small farm. She directs the care of the horses. I love working for her.

She lets me play with power tools. Like chainsaws and weed trimmers and saws and drills and other things that make lots of noise and smell like gas and oil.

She gave me a mission one day—clear the brush from under the electric fence. The brush grows up underneath it, touches the wire, and reduces the current that keeps the horses in the pasture. So off I went, chainsaw and weed trimmer in hand, hacking away at all this undergrowth attacking the fence line. I noticed a sapling growing right under the fence line. I reached for my chainsaw, and just before cranking it, looked back at the sapling and studied its leaves. It was a maple sapling, the kind of tree that blazes orange

41

in the fall, appearing to be on fire in the sunlight; the type of tree that I think is beautiful.

You see, I grew up in a part of the world where pine trees grow like weeds. Pine trees look the same all year long. Hardwoods like maples are rare in that area. Even after all these years of being gone, maples in the fall are a novelty to me.

I put the chainsaw down and picked up my shovel. I decided to dig up the maple sapling and transplant it to another place on the farm where I could enjoy its beauty. I aimed my shovel at the sapling, and just then noticed something growing beside it—poison ivy.

Have you ever touched poison ivy? It causes a miserable itch that lasts for weeks, making you scratch yourself in embarrassing places while in public. I did not want poison ivy.

So, I stood there, thinking about what to do next, when I thought, "There they are: irritating poison ivy and a maple tree destined to be 80 feet or more tall and blaze orange in the fall growing in the same soil, side by side. Something beautiful growing beside something ugly. The best in nature nurtured next to the worst. Something that causes me to praise nature is nestled alongside something to curse about it."

Just doesn't seem right, does it? At least that's what I thought . . .

. . . until I realized that the soil did not care what's planted in it—a maple tree or poison ivy. The soil nourishes and grows whatever it receives.

Your Mind is Like Soil

You can choose to plant poison ivy—only familiar, negative thoughts that erupt in itches of worry that cause you to scratch your head about work. Or, you can choose to plant maple trees—

unfamiliar, positive thoughts that help you attract top talent and reduce team turnover so you create a positive work culture that increases productivity and profit.

Your mind nourishes and grows whatever you focus on.

Your first step to Work Positive is to choose to Perceive the positive at work. Your mind focuses your thoughts every second, and you now know the importance of aiming that focus on the positive work experiences. Your mind craves the familiar, even if it is negative, and you now understand how to carve out new neural pathways in your brain.

The third key aspect to Perceive the positive at work is to filter your thoughts. You turn away from the negative and toward the positive when you focus your thoughts. You search out unfamiliar thoughts when you avoid only familiar thoughts. The reality of work today is that sometimes you turn from a negative thought and run right into another one. You keep turning, only to discover that you are surrounded by negativity. You bump into so much negativity because the company culture is toxic.

What do you do then? You filter your thoughts.

Filters Keep Some Things Out and Let Others Pass Through

Consider your home's heating and air conditioning system. It has a filter that keeps dust out and lets air in. Think about your car's air filter. It catches road dirt and allows the air to pass cleanly so it can mix with the gasoline and power your car. I have a water filter on our home's well. The minerals are caught and the water flows through.

Filters do more than deny the existence of dust, dirt and minerals. They counteract and hold them at bay until the filter becomes full or clogged and someone changes it out for a fresh one.

You direct your mind in the same way. There is too much negativity in the world to deny its existence. Bad things happen in good work cultures daily, and just as perplexing is the reality that good things happen in toxic work cultures daily. To deny that the world is negative is Pollyanna at best and psychotic at worst.

That's why the Work Positive culture is all about why you filter your thoughts rather than deny the existence of negativity at work.

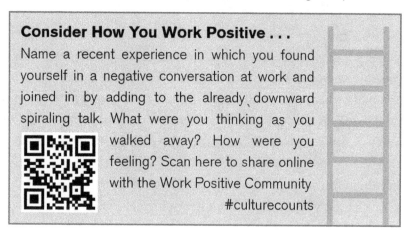

Consider How You Work Positive . . .

Name a recent experience in which you found yourself in a negative conversation at work and joined in by adding to the already downward spiraling talk. What were you thinking as you walked away? How were you feeling? Scan here to share online with the Work Positive Community #culturecounts

What You Resist, Persists

There is an old saying, "What you resist, persists." That is, when you focus your thoughts on not being negative, you concentrate on the "negative" and see past the "not." For example, when you tell yourself, "Now don't forget to . . ." your mind zeroes in on the word "forget." And what do you usually do? Forget it.

When you tell yourself, "Now remember to . . ." your mind takes aim at the word "remember." And what do you usually do? Remember it. It's more than a denial of the negative. It's a filtering of the negative in order to affirm the positive. You focus on the negative as you resist. By filtering it, you acknowledge it and choose the more positive way to think about your work.

My friend, Bob Nicoll, tells the story of walking into a convenience store one hot summer day in Phoenix and seeing a sign above the cash register, "Don't Forget the Ice." He asked the manager how ice sales were. "Slow," the manager said, despite the fact that it was about 110 degrees in the shade.

So, Bob asked for a piece of paper and a magic marker. He created another sign that read, "Remember the Ice." He asked the manager to remove the current sign, put up the new one, and see if that helped sales.

When Bob returned to the store in about three weeks, the manager was so excited to see him. "I've tripled my sales of bags of ice," he said. "And it's all due to your great sign! Thank you!"

What you resist, persists. Poison ivy grows in your work culture. Everyone has customers, teammates, even a boss who irritates us. These poison ivy relationships grow in the same soil as your maple tree relationships. You filter out the poison ivy by refusing to plant it, and when it does grow, by uprooting it and choosing instead to plant and nurture the maple trees. You filter your thoughts to keep out the negative and let the positive pass through into your work. Then you focus on the positive.

Here's how it works. Tons of sand and dirt were moved to replenish the beach while our family vacationed. Pumping in tons of dirt from the ocean floor made the shallow shore water murky and dirty-looking.

Our younger daughter and I went down to check out the water. It was so muddy you couldn't see your feet or anything else even in the shallow water. I said to her, "Yuck! Look how dirty the ocean is."

She said to me, "Daddy, it looks like a chocolate ocean to me."

I looked down at the water again, and this time I saw it. The water really did look chocolate.

My daughter and I looked at the same ocean water with two entirely different perspectives. I saw, "Yuck!" She saw, "Yum!"

She filtered out the obvious, perceived beyond it, and focused on the positive.

You have a choice about what you Perceive at work: yuck or yum. Positive or negative. Your mind grows either one. You choose to Work Positive or work negative.

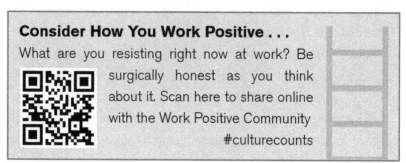

Consider How You Work Positive . . .

What are you resisting right now at work? Be surgically honest as you think about it. Scan here to share online with the Work Positive Community
#culturecounts

Clean Your Filter

A woman and her husband sat at the kitchen table each morning, drinking their coffee and eating their breakfast. One morning, the husband noticed the neighbor's laundry hung out to dry. "Boy," he said, "she sure doesn't know how to wash clothes. They're still dirty." The wife glanced out the window, but said nothing.

The next week, they sat down at the breakfast table again and this time he said, "Well, she learned how to wash clothes. They're bright and clean. Did you say something to her?"

"No, I didn't," said the wife. "But I did clean that window."

Your work filter gets dirty or clogged. It requires cleaning. Like this husband, you develop a critical view of other people and situations when stuck in the familiar negative, and refuse to filter it. Your perception blurs like my vision did in fourth grade when playing baseball and trying to read math problems.

One way to clear up this blurring is to change your perspective. I learned the value of a new perspective as I painted the board fencing around our horse pastures. I bought a five-gallon bucket of stain and lugged it up and down the fence line as I smeared it with my four-inch brush.

Section by section, I painted one side of the fence, and then went to the other side. At one section, the gate was far away and I really didn't want to carry that heavy bucket up the hill to it. So, I came up with the brilliant idea of lifting the bucket up over the fence, putting it down on the other side, and then climbing over the fence myself. Sounds easy enough . . .

. . . until I got the heavy bucket over the top board of the fence, and as it got closer to the ground on the other side and as I stretched further and further to let it down, I tipped it and spilled stain on the ground.

I climbed over the fence and looked at the mess I'd made. Just then, from my new perspective on the other side of the fence, I noticed that the bottom of the fence was high enough for me to have slid the bucket under it instead of lifting it over.

You can imagine what I was thinking—"I wish I had a second chance to do that over."

Do you ever wish for a second chance? A do-over?

Sure you do. You do something. The results are different from what you wanted. You get a new perspective on it and realize what you could have done. Then you want a second chance. You want to unclog your perception filter.

A Great Thing about Your Work Positive Culture

One of the great things about choosing to Work Positive is you discover "do-overs." The mistakes you make deciphering the success code of your work are an expected part of your learning curve. You have an experience like mine. You learn something from a new perspective that helps unstop your filter. Then you find yourself in a similar situation and you do it over, this time with the benefit of what you learned previously. It's a do-over, just like me while painting the fence. What do you think I did the next time I was far away from a gate? I checked out which was better—lift the bucket over the fence or slide it under.

You filter your thoughts, reflecting on previous work experiences and what you can learn from them. That determines what you allow to pass through your filter—the positive—and what you filter out—the negative.

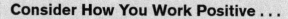

Consider How You Work Positive . . .

What work experience do you wish you could do over? Declare what you learned by writing it down

 in the margin of this page. Scan here to share online with the Work Positive Community

#culturecounts

Filtering in Reverse

So often you allow the negative world to make your decisions, to color your attitude in dark hues of limited options and a lack of optimism rather than filter your thoughts. The negative world offers a reverse filtration of the positive work culture you want.

For instance, it's a rainy Monday. Now what's your typical attitude toward such a day? "No customers will come in today in this kind of weather," you think.

You could just as easily Perceive, "The customers who walk through my door today are ready to buy if they'll come out in this weather."

Now, what if your area is experiencing a drought? What's your attitude?

What if the drought has made the ground hard and the rain is falling so forcefully that it's simply sheeting off, without a real chance for the ground to absorb it? What's your attitude now?

"I bet we'll have a flash flood watch declared and nobody will come in," you might think.

But what would a child see on such a rainy Monday?

- Mud puddles to play in.
- Rivers to stand in and watch the water splash up your legs.
- Boat races with leaves and twigs.
- Bathwater for birds.
- The flowers, grass and trees getting watered.

See how filtering your thoughts makes a positive change in your interpretation of the work culture? What if you allow negative thoughts to pass through and enter your mind without filtering? What happens to your work then?

Imagine for a moment that before you start your car or truck each morning to go to work that you put six grains of sand in your gas tank.

OK, it's only six grains of sand, but if you do it every morning, how long do you think it'll take before your vehicle won't run? Soon, right?

Negative, unpleasant thoughts dropped into your mind affect you in the same way. They break down your mental motor. You're broken down by worry, frustration, and thoughts that your work doesn't matter to anyone. Pretty soon, you're broken down beside the work culture fast lane.

You prevent such tiny grains of negativity from entering your mental engine when you filter your thoughts. You proactively avoid allowing them entrance to your work culture.

Some friends came over to our farm for the first time. The weather was warm enough so that my roses were blooming. As we walked around, one of our friends said, "Your roses are so beautiful! They are gorgeous. I wish I could grow roses."

And yet when I looked at them, I saw the black spot fungus growing on the leaves, turning them yellow, and making them drop off. When I looked at them, I saw the stunted growth of the canes, stunted because of a drought. When I looked at them, I saw what was wrong with the rose bushes, looking right past the beautiful blooms.

The same thing happens as you Perceive your work. You can filter out the negative and look at the beautiful experiences blossoming all around you. The opportunities popping up almost overnight. The resources converging that you imagined. Or, you can bring an unfiltered perception to all the things going wrong at work and the environment around it.

You choose a positive path to success when you filter out the negative perceptions about work.

Or, you invite the negative inside your mind unfiltered and watch yourself sink.

It's your choice.

Your mind grows whatever you plant in it.

Your work grows whatever you plant in it.

Your work growth reflects your mind's growth.

Choose to filter your thoughts and plant the positive and watch your work succeed in ways you can only imagine now.

Grab & Go

Weave your mental filter with these thoughts as you:

1. Plant maple trees in your mind, uproot the poison ivy, and watch your work grow.
2. "What you resist, persists."
3. Perceive the "yum" (chocolate ocean), instead of the "yuck" (murky water) at work.
4. Clean your mind's window often and you'll see clearly how positive your work can grow.
5. Take advantage of "do overs." Plant what you learn into your next work experience.
6. Filter the fuel you pour in your mental motor. Watch as your work speeds up.
7. See the rose blooms at work.

Core Practice 2:

CONCEIVE the POSITIVE at Work

chapter 5

You Can Conceive the Positive at Work

"I think positive. I always think we're going to score.
Two minutes is a lot of time if you have timeouts and
you're throwing every down. I've always had great
receivers, which helps. It's not just me doing it."
—Dan Marino

Y ou began the first core practice to Work Positive, Perceive
the positive at work. You discovered that your mind
naturally focuses. It prefers to focus on the familiar. Yet
you can choose to focus on the unfamiliar and filter your thoughts
to fill your mind with the positive at work.

You want to share these positive thoughts with someone;
to check with another person for confirmation, validation, and
expansion of them.

You are a social human being, born to uncover hidden sources
of positivity with others. Others complete you.

Usually my wife cares for the horses on our farm, but she was out of town one weekend. I volunteered to feed the horses.

It was nightfall when I got home. It was extremely dark with no moon or stars. Also, the area light needed a new bulb and wasn't working.

I poured the feed into the buckets in the barn and headed for the pasture gate. This group of horses is fed outside in black pails on the ground. They like to play with their black pails and roll them around the pasture.

I stepped through the gate, hooked it behind me, and started looking for those black pails on the ground on a dark night. The horses heard me muttering to myself, "Now where are those pails? And why isn't there any light out here?" They knew my presence means feeding time so they galloped up beside me, wondering why I didn't just put the feed in the pails and get out of their way.

So, here I am searching in the dark for pails, jostled by horses who just want to eat. I started dancing around the pasture, trying to keep the horses from stepping on my feet, which of course means they started dancing around trying not to step on my feet.

Now It's comical. Then not so much.

Finally, I thought to myself, "Instead of stumbling around the pasture with horses chasing you for feed, let the horses show you where the pails are."

So, I stopped my dancing, stood perfectly still, and told the horses to "Go on." Then I watched as they went and stood in various places around the pasture. I walked up to each one and discovered a black pail on the ground in front of them, poured in the feed, and moved on to the next one. The horses could see the pails when I couldn't. I let them guide me.

Do you ever find yourself stumbling around in the negative darkness at work for something positive? We all do. We need some help from others.

You took the first step to Perceive the positive at work. You focus on the positive and filter out the negative to create a Work Positive culture. Like me with the horses, you know what you want to do with your thoughts, and yet, realize you need someone else's experiences, knowledge, and network.

Sure, I had the feed the horses wanted, but I didn't know how best to deliver it. They knew how the feed was to be delivered. I partnered with the horses, and together we got them fed. And I kept all of my toes intact.

Consider How You Work Positive . . .

When was the last time you became anxious about getting something done? So anxious that you tried to accomplish the task alone, without the benefit of the people around you, some of whom knew what to do? How did that work out for you? Scan here to share online with the Work Positive Community #culturecounts

---

The second core practice to Work Positive is to Conceive the positive at work. Conception requires at least two people. This is the social dynamic of your Work Positive culture.

chapter 6

Cooperate Completely

*"Great discoveries and improvements invariably involve the
cooperation of many minds. I may be given credit for having
blazed the trail, but when I look at the subsequent developments
I feel the credit is due to others rather than to myself."*
— Alexander Graham Bell

You were created to Work Positive with others.

Your success depends on you attracting customers
and clients, teammates and suppliers with whom you can
Conceive. Your first step is to Conceive the positive at work by
cooperating completely with others.

Cooperation challenges the familiar notions of achieving
positive success as a self-made person, pulling yourself up by your
own bootstraps. This notion is a myth. You have benefited from
conceiving the positive with others since before you can remember.

Do you remember your mother and father getting up at 2:00
AM to feed you? Can you recall when you were an infant in a crib,
screaming your head off because your stomach growled, and all of
a sudden, this bleary-eyed person appeared over your crib, reached

down, picked you up, and held you close? You felt warm in that embrace. You heard a soft voice. You were fed. The next thing you knew, you fell asleep again, back in your crib, totally satisfied and happy. Do you remember that experience?

Of course not. These gracious acts of kindness happened night after night for months and months, depriving your parents of much-needed sleep, and you have no memory of them.

And yet they still happened.

What about other gracious acts others have done for you that you can't remember?

Some of them were done without your knowledge. A sippy cup of water given in the middle of the night to help with a bad dream. Long hours worked to buy you new clothes. Prayers offered for your safety as you drove away from home for the first time.

All of these acts combined to make you who you are today—a wonderful, unique human being capable of a Work Positive culture through relationships.

However alone you may feel at times at work, someone is with you. You were created to be in cooperative relationships with others. You have not arrived at your current mile marker as a solo driver. You traveled in a carpool the whole time.

Consider How You Work Positive . . .

Remember a time of struggle or challenge in your work, a time your thoughts were more negative, like, "I'm all alone in this," or "There's no one who can help me with this problem." Who appeared to help? How did this person assist you? Scan here to share online with the Work Positive Community #culturecounts

Who Do You Lean On?

In our yard was a stand of pines. Their limbs had grown together. Also, in our yard was one pine growing by itself.

A snowfall came and the ice and snow lay heavy on the branches of those pines. The weight bent the branches down toward the ground; so low that in the stand of pines, the branches from one tree were on the trunk and branches of another. None of the branches broke because the trees leaned their branches on one another.

The pine that grew by itself did less well. There were no other trees to lean against, so the lone pine's branches became so heavy they broke. The tree uprooted under the weight and was later removed.

Like the pines, you're stronger and live longer when surrounded by others. The people around you—customers/clients, teammates/boss, family/friends, and vendors/suppliers—are there for you to lean on when the weight of work is too much for you to stand alone. These people are your team. I like to think of mine as "Team Joey."

You were created to cooperate completely with others at work.

I discovered this creative nature of relationships as I pulled up to a bank drive-in and found an open lane. It was my first time using this bank's drive-through service. I'm accustomed to the ones that have the round container that open at one end, you throw your stuff in, close it, place it back on the tube, and push the button.

This one was different. It had a blue box and no buttons. Well, the box I figured out and placed it back on the tube. The sign read, "Autoconveyor" so I thought you just put it back and away it goes. I placed the box back, but nothing happened.

I looked at the person in the vehicle beside me, smiled, and hoped they didn't see what I couldn't do.

Just then, a voice came on the intercom and said, "Please push the box up a little." I did and away it went.

We all need a little help occasionally. For you to Conceive and Work Positive, you reach out for a little help from your friends. Sometimes you get it whether you reach out or not.

A couple arrived at an automobile dealership to pick up their car. They were told that the keys were locked in it. So, they went to the service department and found a mechanic working feverishly to unlock the driver's side door.

As the wife watched from the passenger's side door, she instinctively tried the door handle and discovered it was open. "Hey," she told the mechanic, "it's open!"

"I know," he said, "I already got that side."

Can you relate?

Yes, we all have days like this.

Consider How You Work Positive . . .

When was the last time you got so involved in a work task that you lost sight of the big picture? How did someone come along and help you? How did this person cooperate with you to Conceive the positive? Scan here to share online with the Work Positive Community

#culturecounts

Something You Miss

Cooperating completely with your teammates or manager, customers or clients to Work Positive presupposes that you are incomplete alone, and complete with others. Sometimes, your ego gets in the way of your working best from the Conceive core practice. Part of the challenge may be that you're really good at so many and varied tasks that you buy the lie you can do it all. And you might can . . . just not all at once.

The truth is if you passionately want to Work Positive, you must redefine your egotistical reality of "I already know that" to "Please show me how."

One day a blue block of frozen material crashed from the sky into a farmer's field. He cut off a chunk of it, put it in his freezer, and called the sheriff. He was convinced it was something extraterrestrial, but all he really knew was it stunk when it melted. The sheriff examined it and didn't have a clue, so he called a chemistry professor from the local college. The professor took a sample from it and left with the promise to analyze it in her lab and call back with the results. The farmer kept the blue frozen material in his freezer, making sure that it was carefully preserved. He just knew he had discovered the key to life in an alien universe.

The chemistry professor called the farmer. "Sir," she said, "your blue frozen material is definitely not extraterrestrial so you can relax. But please take it out of your freezer and throw it away as soon as possible."

"Why?" the farmer asked.

"Because, sir," she said, "what you have in your freezer is the portable toilet fluid ejected from a plane."

One of the most essential ingredients of your cooperating with others to Work Positive is that no matter how much you Perceive, and think you Perceive accurately, there is something someone else knows more about than you do. The reality of work today is you can use some help.

The good news is you have it. You are in relationships with others to receive everything you require to Work Positive.

Think about the Wildflowers

I have a friend who worked in the family business for most of his adult life. Sure, he operated as a business owner, but his father started the business. It was his father who spent sleepless nights worrying about making payroll and whether his suppliers would extend credit again. My friend was insulated from such anxieties…

…until the family business was sold, and he started his own business. He became an entrepreneur really for the first time. Over lunch one day, he talked about being on the "front line" of his business, from the ground up, and the pressures he was enduring. Particularly troublesome for him was what he called "financial terror"—the compilation of concerns about cash flow, credit, profit margins, etc. Not knowing if there would be enough to support his family in the lifestyle to which they were accustomed kept him up late at night and woke him each morning.

As a business owner, I told him that I can relate with his "financial terror." He asked me, "How do you deal with it?"

I told him about the daylilies growing in beds along the driveway to our home. Through drought and monsoon, they just keep growing and even show up in places where I didn't plant them. I really don't do much for them except keep as many weeds away as I can. For years now they continue to grow without my really caring for them. Their orange and yellow, maroon and pink colors make outstanding borders. About all I do is transplant a few in the fall.

Then I told him about all the varieties of birds with whom my wife and I share our farm. There are bluebirds, geese, crows, goldfinches, hawks, owls, wrens, sparrows, cardinals, whippoorwills, swallows, martins, woodpeckers, and the list goes on. We feed them in the winter when the snow covers the ground. They eat the mosquitoes and other bugs that would drive us indoors in the spring. Their songs greet us in the mornings, carry us through the days, and put us to bed at night. We do very little for them and yet they brighten our world.

I told him that since daylilies and birds receive everything they require, it's logically consistent that everything we need to Work Positive arrives on time.

There really is enough to go around.

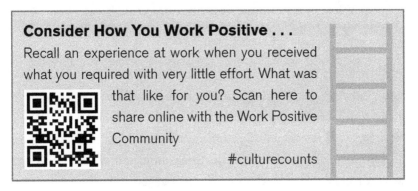

Consider How You Work Positive . . .
Recall an experience at work when you received what you required with very little effort. What was that like for you? Scan here to share online with the Work Positive Community

#culturecounts

Who Do You Attract?

Conceiving your Work Positive culture consists of more than just your efforts to generate positivity. You are in relationships already that validate, confirm, and even expand how you Work Positive. You literally were born for these relationships, created to cooperate completely. Working from these relationships is the key to how you Conceive a Work Positive culture.

The key to leveraging these relationships is to focus and filter your thoughts in such a way that you become the kind of person that you want to Work Positive with. This is how you attract the persons you prefer as customers/clients, teammates/bosses, and vendors/suppliers.

Ask yourself three questions as you become that person who attracts Work Positive partners with whom to best Conceive:

1. What are my core values, i.e., those character traits that I want to exhibit in my work relationships? What would my family members say are my core values?

2. What are my work priorities, i.e., those matters that I consider most important for my work behavior? How do my calendar and to-do list reflect these priorities?

3. What is my unique contribution to make at work? That "thing" that my company and teammates look to me to do?

You literally attract people with whom you share core values and priorities, and those to whom you contribute uniquely. This attraction factor is a key determiner of how you Conceive to Work Positive with team members and customers alike. By focusing on and filtering your thoughts, you choose how you Work Positive to attract top talent and reduce team turnover so you create a positive work culture that increases productivity and profits. Your choices shape the magnetic predisposition for selecting those people with whom you best Conceive. For example, if you Conceive your work more positively, you attract similarly dispositioned people. Those who resonate on this frequency are literally drawn to you because of your common work pitch.

Conversely, you find people coming to work with you who are more negative if your work is grounded there. They vibrate on a negative pitch and are drawn to you on that frequency.

Like attracts like at work.

Your best work is as you cooperate with others. You resemble those with whom you share common core values and priorities who will receive your unique contribution. Your work pitch broadcasts vibrations that resonate with similarly tuned persons whether customers or teammates.

Do you ever complain about your customers? They don't pay their bills on time, or maybe they're constantly trying to get something for nothing. Who attracted them to do business with you?

What about your teammates? Ever hear yourself saying something like, "You just can't find good help these days" or "Nobody wants to want work anymore"? Who attracted them?

What about your boss? Do you ever say, "How in the world does anybody work for him?" or "If I can find another job, I'm out of here!"? Who decided to work there?

A great question to ask yourself is, "How am I attracting these people? What is there about who I am that draws them to me?"

One of the greatest challenges in understanding how the Conceive core practice is realizing that like attracts like. These people onto whom you shift responsibility for your challenges work with you because you chose them. You attracted them by way of your core values, priorities, and unique contribution.

You can attract others to your team who share your positive direction. Those who choose to Work Positive find their way to you. The attraction factor is extremely strong, and the research proves it.

In 1948, Boston University and a research team began a heart disease project searching for indicators that predict heart attacks. Over 12,000 persons from three generations have participated. The results are fascinating not only in predicting heart attacks, but also in proving the undeniable nature of how you attract others.

Obesity is a direct correlative to heart attacks. The Framingham Heart Study found that obese people attract each other, and that if you are not obese, and associate with obese persons, you are about 171 percent more likely to become obese yourself.

Associating with individuals who have unhealthy eating habits creates the context in which your nutrition behavior changes. The attraction factor changes the physical characteristics of those attracted.

Divorce is a major life stressor. Researchers studying the effects of divorce on heart attacks also discovered that if you spend time with a large number of divorced persons, you are about 147 percent more likely to divorce yourself.

Your view of your spouse becomes jaundiced if you work in an office with people who chronically complain about their spouses, or ex-spouses. Remember: you see what you look for. You become impatient with your spouse's shortcomings and look for greener grass on the other side of the bed rather than staying home and fertilizing your own.

It's up to you to attract positive teammates, customers, and others with whom to work.

Ask for Hope that Helps

It's also up to you to let go of any need you might have to do all the work yourself, thinking that it's easier for you to do it yourself than to involve others. You ask for and accept help from others as you Conceive to Work Positive.

When our older daughter was two years old, she was intent on doing things for herself. "I do it, Daddy," she would tell me and then she would try to open the door, even though she could hardly reach the knob and the door weighed more than her. Or, she would try to make a puzzle piece fit upside down.

Sometimes, she couldn't do it. Still she kept trying until she became so frustrated her words came out slightly off. She would say, "Hope me, Daddy," meaning, "Help me, Daddy."

"OK, I'll help you," I would say. "Let's pull on the door together" or "Let's turn the puzzle piece another way and try it." She and I together would do what she failed to do alone.

You'll try to do something that you think you can do on your own at work. "I do it," you'll say. Frustration is the soil in which the realization grows that you can use the hope that help brings. That's when this core practice focuses you to attract positive team members who want to help.

Asking for hope that helps draws to you other hopeful people who help. Like the daylilies and birds, you receive what you require to Work Positive in a negative world.

You gain much-needed information about frozen blue chunks, locked automobiles, autoconveyors, and anything else there is a knowledge gap. You discover customers and clients, teammates and employees to lean on when work turns cold. You recall that you were fed, clothed, and cared for in ways that you fail to remember.

Become the teammate you desire to work with. Attract those with whom you can redefine your reality, Conceive how you will Work Positive, and make your dreams come true.

Consider How You Work Positive . . .

List your core values, priorities, and unique work contribution to the world. Make a list of people with whom you share some of the above. Scan here to share online with the Work Positive Community #culturecounts

You Conceive the positive to attract top talent, reduce team turnover so you create a positive work culture that increases productivity and profits.

Grab & Go

Conceive these significant, positive thoughts as you "Cooperate Completely":

1. You and your work arrived at your current mile marker as more than a solo driver. You rode in a carpool the whole time.
2. The pine that stood by itself broke. We have each other to lean on as we Work Positive.
3. There is always something you miss regardless of how accurately you Perceive your work . . . like the farmer and the chemistry professor.
4. You can use some help at work. The good news is you have it.
5. Think about the daylilies and the birds the next time work goes negative.
6. Define your core values, priorities, and unique contribution to make at work. You attract customers and clients, vendors and suppliers, teammates and bosses with whom you share these qualities.
7. Ask, "Hope me" instead of saying, "I do it."

chapter 7

Compare and Compete Rarely

"It's hard to soar like an eagle when you're flying with a bunch of turkeys."
—A bumper sticker

A duck hunter in town had the best retriever in the county. He refused to take anyone hunting with him to see the dog work. Finally, he agreed to let one friend go with his promise not to tell anyone in town about his dog.

The friend promised, and so off they went duck hunting. He shot a duck, and the dog took off to retrieve the downed bird. The dog walked on the water to the downed bird, picked it up, and returned it, still walking on the water, to the hunters.

The owner of the dog turned to his partner and said, "Now do you understand why I don't want you to tell anyone in town about my dog?"

"Yes, I do," the fellow replied. "I wouldn't want anybody to know I owned a dog that couldn't swim, either."

So, how do you Conceive your work with others—as a dog that walks on water? Or as a dog that can't swim?

Dogs that Didn't Swim

One of the largest challenges you face as you Work Positive is attracting positive people with whom to Conceive. Attracting top talent and reducing team turnover are formidable barriers as The Great Resignation proves.

Your core values, priorities, and unique contribution attract those who resonate with you regardless of how and where you serve in the company. Your work amplifies these three vibrations regardless of where you are in the organization. Work negative and negative individuals find their way in your front door as customers and teammates. Think of them as "Negative Conceivers."

There are some notable examples. Ken Olsen, founder of Digital Equipment, said in 1977, "There is no reason anyone would want a computer in their home."

A Western Union Telegraph Company internal memo in 1876 read, "This 'telephone' has too many shortcomings to be seriously considered as a means of communication."

Gary Cooper said when he turned down the lead role in *Gone with the Wind*, "I'm just glad it'll be Clark Gable who's falling on his face and not Gary Cooper."

In 1962 Decca Recording Company rejected the Beatles after a studio session, reportedly because "We don't like their sound, and guitar music is on the way out."

"Negative Conceivers" are everywhere. The reality is that unguided, most of us stumble down negative pathways and like Ken Olsen, Western Union, Gary Cooper, and Decca Records, miss the mark.

So how much power will you give them these Negative Conceivers?

Will you follow their lead into dead-ends that block your working more from the Conceive core practice? The temptation is to give away your personal choice to focus on the positive thoughts and people and filter out the negative.

Jim Rohn was fond of saying, "You are the average of the five persons with whom you spend the most time."

Think about it this way: what if Michael Dell chose to Conceive with Ken Olsen? Or, what if Bell had taken to heart Western Union's analysis of his telephone? Or, what if Clark Gable had said, "Gary Cooper is right. I'm turning down this role"? Or, what if John, Paul, George, and Ringo accepted at face value Decca Records' assessment, packed their guitars, and went back home to Liverpool?

Your laptop and tablet, iPhone and smartphone, classic movie choices, and music selections would disappear quickly.

How Much Personal Power Do You Give to Drowning Dogs?

The reality of work today is that you pursue negative pathways at times. You miss the mark just as these prominent persons and companies did. However, you have an incredible choice about how much personal power to give away to others as you Conceive.

An airline pilot hammered his plane into the runway during a landing. His airline required him to stand in the door while the passengers exited, smile, and thank them for flying. He really didn't want to do this since his landing was anything but smooth.

Finally, everyone had gotten off the plane except for this little old lady with a cane. The pilot breathed a sigh of relief until the lady asked him, "Sonny, mind if I ask a question?"

"Why no, ma'am," said the pilot. "What is it?"

She asked, "Did we land or were we shot down?"

Sometimes your best efforts at landing fail. You get shot down and want to avoid facing others. It is in these moments that you discover the kind of persons whom you attracted at work. Positive people encourage you to recover, remind you that mistakes are expected, and help you back up. Negative people discourage you, ridicule you for even trying, and drop you.

Everyone attracts negative people at some point in the work journey. You are remembering some of them now...

...regardless of their actual names, think of them as Eeyore Vampires. Eeyore is the character who, when Winnie the Pooh, Piglet, or Tigger would suggest some positive playday pursuit, said, "It'll never work."

They're Vampires because at night they disturb your sleep with worry and zap your energy for the next workday. At night, they call your home and distract your attention away from your family. They circle your thoughts and suck your time, energy, and attention.

You know these Eeyore Vampires.

You wish they would just go away.

You know they won't.

Everyone confronts Eeyore Vampires.

How much power will you give these Eeyore Vampires?

The real challenge for you at work is that the Eeyore Vampires who are teammates, customers, suppliers aren't just cuddly cartoon characters from a children's book.

What about the teammate who expresses a negative opinion about you to his co-workers? How much time do you give to recovering your relationships with teammates?

Or, what about the negative customer who throws a wet blanket on everything you try to do to please her with excellent customer service? How much energy do you waste on she-who-won't-be-pleased?

And what about the supplier who tells all the other competing vendors that you exclusively do business with him, preventing you from receiving the best bids? How much of your attention does he get?

Do You Compare and Compete?

The real challenge is you begin to compare and compete when you allow Eeyore Vampires to have such a negative influence on you. You embrace a scarcity mindset based on a negative view that says, "There is not enough to go around. I got mine. You get yours." The Conceive core practice roots best in the soil of cooperation. Cooperation grows in abundance; that working together "we" can achieve more than "me." To cooperate is to acknowledge that there is more than enough to go around for all.

You assume a superior-inferior relationship when you compare and compete. You buy the lie that, "Since I can accumulate more than you, I must be a better person."

Hear the compare and compete mentality driven by insecurity?

Eeyore Vampires at work compare amounts of whatever you prize, and compete for more in an effort to prop up an insecure ego. Eeyore Vampires bite and infect you with the power to reverse the osmosis of your Perceive filter so you focus on the negative and filter out the positive.

You work negative. Top talent refuses to come to work with you. Team members leave and fail to come back. Forget about creating a positive work culture. Oh, and those are profits circling the company bowl.

Eeyore Vampires are contagious. They are deadly.

Think about it this way. I have a favorite pair of blue jeans that I enjoy working in around the farm. I've snagged and ripped them on numerous occasions, so much so that some of the holes are pretty large. Let's say that I want to salvage these jeans and patch them. What would you think if I choose to patch them with some of the finest silk from Hong Kong?

I've lost my mind, right?

Or, let's say that my home is falling down. The foundation is crumbling on the north end. Therefore, my door jambs are tilting and the doors won't close. The floors are uneven and I trip on the hardwood boards sticking up. I decide to add on to my home and spend $200,000 building an addition off the sagging back porch. What would you think of my remodeling?

I'm the dimmest bulb in the pack, eh?

Or, what if instead of adding on to my falling down home, I decide to build a new home. I have a choice between building on a sandy stretch of beach, where a hurricane has come on shore three times in the last ten years, or at the base of a mountain on top of a granite slab that extends for miles underground. Which site should I choose?

But I really like the beach . . .

Or, let's say that I'm blind and traveling to an unfamiliar city. I choose as my traveling companion a woman who also happens to be blind. She has never been to this city either, and offers to act as my guide. Should I go with her?

All of these make about as much sense as when you allow Eeyore Vampires to infect you with a compare and compete mentality. It is the same as patching denim with silk, or adding on to a dilapidated dwelling, or building on weather-stricken sand, or letting the blind lead the blind.

A Better Way to Work

There is a better way to work.

Wayne Dyer told then-*Success* editor Darren Hardy a story about H.L. Mencken, a newspaper columnist in the 1900s. Many of his columns provoked negative response letters. He wrote a column that basically responded: "I have your letters in hand. I am sitting in the smallest room in my home. Soon they will be behind me."

Mencken detached himself from the negativity and chose to kick the Eeyore Vampires to the curb.

How much energy and attention do you give to worrying about what Eeyore Vampires think about your work? When you buy their lie, you are complicit in their conspiracy to suck the Work Positive culture out of you.

The better way is to seek out teams of positive people. Deny the negative Eeyore Vampires your positive time, energy, and attention. Put them behind you like Mencken. Refuse to rent them space in your mind and relationships. Restrict their stealing minutes from your time. Their compare and compete version of work debilitates your attracting top talent, reducing team turnover, and creating a positive work culture that increases productivity and profits.

A coaching client came to our farm so he could spend some time away from the compare and compete world of his business and Conceive with me. It was the fall of the year and as we walked and talked down our driveway, we stopped beside a section of fence along a horse pasture. The sun was setting, casting its last rays of the day on the woods. The setting sun focused like a spotlight on a maple tree, its brilliant orange colors looked like fire. My client noticed the tree.

Earlier we talked about the compare and compete nature of work; of how critical others were of him and the professional barbs that became personal injuries he sustained by listening and taking their negativity to heart. As we stood there, leaning on the fence, soaking in the brilliance of the maple tree in the setting sun's rays, I noticed that the tree beside the maple was a cedar. The cedar was easily overlooked when compared to the maple.

"Look at the cedar tree beside the maple," I said. "What do you see?"

"It doesn't look as good as the maple beside it," he said.

"But the cedar is still a cedar." I said. "It doesn't care at all. It's just standing there, being a cedar tree, without any need to compare itself to the maple."

"It's just being a cedar and letting the maple be itself," he said. "I can do that."

Compare and compete rarely and Work Positive as who you are. You do you. Free others in the company to do the same. Stop comparing and competing. Start cooperating as you and your teammates Conceive the positive at work. Everyone wins as top talent is attracted, team turnover reduces, and a positive work culture increases productivity and profits!

Compare and compete rarely.

Focus on the positive people at work and filter out the Eeyore Vampires. As you cooperate often and compare and compete rarely, then you are ready to Conceive more of your Work Positive culture on the ultimate level—you Collaborate with others.

Grab & Go

As you "Compare and Compete Rarely," remember:

1. Conceive your work with positive people who see the dog walking on water.
2. You have a choice about how much work power you give away to Eeyore Vampires.
3. You embrace a scarcity mindset based on a negative view of reality that says, "There is not enough to go around in the universe. I got mine. You get yours" when you compare and compete.
4. Seek out teams of positive people. Deny the Eeyore Vampires your positive energy.
5. Build your work on positive granite.
6. Sometimes you're the cedar. Other times, you're the maple. Be fine as both.
7. You do you. Free others to do the same.

chapter 8

Collaborate with Others

"I believe that you should gravitate to people who are doing productive and positive things with their lives."
—Nadia Comaneci

Someone did an experiment with two groups of golfers. Each group had a round of golf videotaped.

The video of the rounds was edited. The first group watched a video of their best shots—their longest drives, their most accurate iron shots and chips, their one-putts. The instructor praised the golfers and told them to "go out there and play like this again." So, the golfers did. They improved their scores.

The second group watched a video of their worst shots— their drives that were topped, their shots that were hooked and chips that went over the greens, their missed short putts. The instructor told these golfers, "People, is this any way to play golf? Now go out there and fix those shots." So, the golfers went out and played worse than before.

To which group of golfers would you prefer to belong?

The first group, of course.

The first group Conceived their shots positively. Not only did their instructor cooperate with them to remind them of their most successful shots, but she collaborated with them. Knowing that they would play better after viewing their best strokes, she cooperated by shooting video of those shots, and then took their play to the next level by encouraging them. The instructor and the golfers partnered successfully.

Conception Takes Two

This Conceive core practice coaches you to focus on positive people and filter out the negative ones. This social dynamic requires at least two. By nature, conception requires two persons contributing to the outcome. Basic biology, right? At least two people contribute positively to an outcome that is more successful than either one of them could achieve alone. They positively work together for the mutual benefit of one another and others.

For example, we had just tucked our younger daughter in for a good night's sleep when a thunderstorm blew up. The wind whistled. The lightning flashed. The thunder rattled the windows.

I heard all this sound-and-light show from downstairs in my recliner. Between the "booms" I heard this muffled voice calling, "Daddy! Daddy!" So, I went upstairs to our younger daughter's bedroom where I found her with the covers pulled up over her head.

"What's wrong?" I asked.

"I'm scared of the thunder," she said. "Will you lie down with me?"

"Sure," I said as I got under the covers. "But why does it help with me under the covers?"

"Because the thunder can't hurt me when you're here. You're my Daddy," she said.

Work gets pretty scary sometimes, too.

Who You Gonna Call?

You reach out to the person with whom you successfully collaborated at some point in the past. She keeps your perspective on the long view, not the short term, when she's around. You are a better person when around him because he brings out the best in you and encourages you to do what you can.

You bring out the best in one another as you share common core values and the priorities of the Work Positive culture. You encourage one another's unique contribution at work. Collaboration happens as you filter out the Eeyore Vampires and focus on cooperating with positive people who have abilities that are complementary to yours. You avoid attracting the ones who tell you, "It'll never work," and instead say, "Let's talk about how this can work."

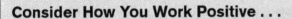

Consider How You Work Positive . . .

Who brings out the best in you? How much time do you spend with this person? How can you enjoy more time with this person? Scan here to share online with the Work Positive Community

#culturecounts

They show you your best, most successful work shots and encourage you to do it some more in the next quarter. That's the Conceive core practice of your Work Positive culture at the ultimate level—collaboration.

Who Brightens Your Day?

One fall, I planted some daffodils in front of a rose bed. They came up, bravely lifting their golden heads to see if winter really was gone and spring had come. They started timidly at first, just barely pushing up a green leaf or two. Then as they survived, more and more leaves emerged, until finally those golden heads shone through.

I noticed something really interesting. Our home shades the daffodils from all the eastern, morning sun. Not a ray gets through. The afternoon, western sun gets completely through, bathing the daffodils daily.

As the daffodils' golden flowers popped through, guess which way they faced? That's right, every single one of them turned its cup towards the western sun.

Where does the warm light come from that nourishes you at work?

Who are the people that brighten your Zoom calls?

How can you collaborate with them more?

The daffodils enjoyed a collaborative relationship with the sun. They cooperated with one another without any need for comparison or competition. It cost the sun nothing to light up the daffodils. It simply went about its normal activities as the sun. The daffodils did what they were created to do—soaked up the sun rays.

The same is true of your work and the people you attract to it. You Conceive best as you collaborate.

It's Your Choice

You choose the people with whom you Conceive at work. You choose your customers and clients, your boss and teammates. Selecting those who bring out the best in you and in whom you bring out the best is essential.

One of the challenges is avoiding the isolationism that the compare-and-compete paradigm births in you. There are others who want to help you Achieve more at work. You become aware that you attract people to your work, look around at who you're attracting, and invite the ones who want to collaborate to carry the workload with you. You must seek out and ask to collaborate.

A young son and his dad walked through the woods one day.

They approached a large rock and the little fellow said, "Hey Dad! Do you think I can lift that rock?"

"Of course you can," the dad said, "if you use all your strength."

The boy squatted down over the rock, put his hands around it, took a deep breath, and pulled on it as hard as he could. He failed to budge the rock even one inch.

Then he took an even deeper breath, and pulled on the rock even harder, grunting with all his might. Still the rock did not budge.

"I thought you said I could move this rock," the son said as he stood up next to his Dad.

"I did," the father replied, "but you didn't use all your strength."

The boy was indignant. "Yes, I did," he said. "I gave it all I had."

"But you didn't use all your strength," the dad insisted. "You could have asked me for help."

Ego paints you into a corner of isolation with no viable exit. You make a mess of work when you sequester yourself from others with whom you could collaborate. You refuse to use all your strength which lies beyond yourself, within those close by who are ready to Work Positive. The impossible becomes possible as you move your workloads in collaborative relationships.

Knowing Them When You See Them

How do you recognize these persons with whom you best collaborate and Conceive the positive at work?

There are five key characteristics to look for in people whom you attract. These are the people who choose to create a Work Positive culture that attracts top talent and reduces team turnover so you increase productivity and profits.

Think of these five key characteristics as what you look for in a Work Positive Dream Team member that is beyond the resume. If you interview for positions, develop open-ended questions that measure for each. If you are on a team, think of topics you can discuss and responses to look for in all kinds of conversations that reveal these qualities.

These five key characteristics determine the extent to which your work culture supports Work Positive Dream Teams. Discover them. Develop them. Dialogue about them.

Listen

The first characteristic you look for is they listen.

What if you visit your medical doctor because you're sick? The nurse walks in, takes your temperature and blood pressure, asks you what's wrong, writes it down on your chart, and says, "The doctor will be in to see you in a moment."

And pretty soon the doctor walks in, reading your chart, and never looks up at you. He doesn't ask you what's wrong, where you hurt, how long you've been sick, "How 'bout that Tom Brady? Think he'll ever retire?" Nothing.

All of a sudden he writes something down and says, "OK, I understand what's wrong with you. Here's a prescription. Pay at the window," and walks out.

Would you believe that doctor understands your condition?

Why not?

The doctor failed to listen to understand.

There is a line in the movie *Pulp Fiction* that goes something like this: "Are you really listening, or just waiting to talk?"

Narcissism is a symptom of a compare-and-compete work culture. Listening to another to the point of understanding is one of the hallmark qualities of someone with whom you want to Work Positive. This person expects to collaborate. Such a person refuses any claim to know all the answers to your work questions without consultation. Instead they ask rather than assume and seek to collaborate through active listening.

My Grandfather Greene was just such a man. He was an entrepreneur—a crop farmer, dairy farmer, and proprietor of a country store—who understood the importance of collaboration. Once he bought a field on which to grow his crops. He learned everything he could about the field before making the purchase.

When he completed the purchase, another man who lived near the property approached my Grandfather as he worked the land. After exchanging their pleasantries, the man said to my Grandfather, "You know this is a hail field, don't you?"

"No," my Grandfather said. "What do you mean it's a hail field?"

"Well," the man said, "when the thunderstorms roll through here, and they do pretty often, the worst of the weather hits this field. I don't know why, but when we have hail over here, it's always on this field."

My Grandfather thanked the man for the information. The next day, he called his insurance agent and purchased twice the amount of insurance with which he normally secured a property and crops, based on the man's observation.

The man was correct. If it hailed anywhere nearby, it hailed on that field, destroying the crops. My Grandfather was prepared. He covered his investment well because he listened to the other man and understood. People with whom you Conceive the positive at work collaborate and listen to understand.

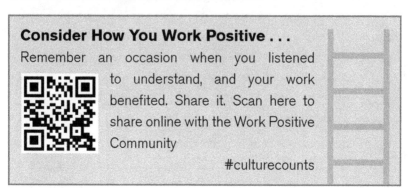

Consider How You Work Positive . . .
Remember an occasion when you listened to understand, and your work benefited. Share it. Scan here to share online with the Work Positive Community

#culturecounts

Humility

A second key characteristic of a Work Positive Dream Team with whom you can collaborate is humility. You know humble people. Such persons think more about you and less about themselves. They hang on your every word. They look you in the eye. They pause when you finish talking, absorbing your words, the tones and inflections behind them.

Others refuse to listen and wait impatiently to talk. They jump in and talk mostly about themselves and their accomplishments when you take a breath. Their narcissism is evident.

Humble people understand how collaborative, Work Positive Dream Teams function. They speak of others and their contribution to achieving the impossible when thrust into the limelight. They talk about the team and "we" and avoid "me" and "I."

We see such humility in NASCAR racing. Thousands of fans crowd into luxury boxes and "chicken bone" seats just to watch their favorite drivers go as fast as they can around oval tracks, yelling and screaming at the top of their lungs, cheering them on. The drivers are the real celebrities here, making millions of dollars not just running cars, but endorsing everything from soft drinks to motor oil. The drivers make the headlines. It's the drivers who show up on a box of Wheaties. You can name at least one of these drivers, I bet . . . but can you name a tire changer?

You see, while all this high-profile, big-money activity is going on, down in the pits is a team of guys whom no one asks to endorse anything. They'll never get their faces on anybody's box of cereal. Yet the driver is dead on the track without this team of guys working together to change tires, fill gas tanks, make track bar adjustments, and clean windshields.

As it is with that driver, so it is with you and your work. You belong to a team of people helping the company go around daily. The humble can name these teams—teammates and leaders, managers and suppliers, customers and clients—who keep the business going. make "the team" a dream team.

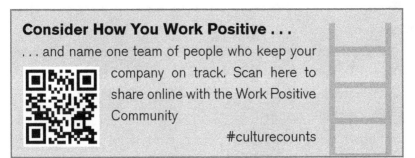

Consider How You Work Positive . . .

. . . and name one team of people who keep your company on track. Scan here to share online with the Work Positive Community

#culturecounts

Mutual Benefit

A third key characteristic of those persons you attract and choose to collaborate with as a Work Positive Dream Team is, they work for mutual benefit. They share accomplishments, both the credit and the rewards. They genuinely care as much for your success as they do their own.

As you know, I really don't like squirrels because they steal the seed we put out for the birds. I read about and bought a weight-sensitive bird feeder called "The Absolute." The Century Tool & Manufacturing Co. of Cherry Valley, Illinois, made it with a counterweight device that shuts the feeder door when anything heavier than a bird lights on the feeder. When it first came on the market, Sue Wells, director of the National Bird-Feeding Society, says she and others thought someone "had finally come up with the ultimate solution."

The squirrels on our little farm have defeated this most ingenious device by working for mutual benefit. While one squirrel stands on the counterweight bar behind the feeder, keeping the front door from shutting, the other squirrel stands on the roost and feeds. Then they switch places.

These squirrels understand mutual benefit. If they can Work Positive for each other's mutual benefit, maybe you and your team can, too.

People with whom you want to Conceive your Work Positive Dream Team choose mutual benefit. It is one of their core values and priorities. It drives the unique contribution they offer to create a Work Positive culture.

Consider How You Work Positive . . .

Who is someone with whom you have worked for mutual benefit? What is that person's role—

 teammate or boss, customer or client, or something else? Scan here to share online with the Work Positive Community

#culturecounts

These are the people you want to attract, choose, and invite onto your Work Positive Dream Team.

Accountability

A fourth characteristic of people with whom to collaborate on your Work Positive Dream Team is they hold you accountable. They bring out the best in you by asking questions that help you be surgically honest with yourself. Such questions create a healthy amount of pressure that pushes you toward those habits and patterns that shape work for success.

Think about a rubber band that has a certain shape. You pick up the rubber band and stretch it out and around a stack of cards. The band has changed its shape in response to the stack of cards and the pressure you put on it to fit. The band maintains that shape as long as it is around the cards. Relieve the pressure by taking it off the cards and what happens? It goes back to its original shape.

You work like that rubber band. Accountability serves to exert best-inducing pressure in collaborative relationships. One of the reasons you are at your best with another person is the give-and-take of such relationships, the encouragement to do and be better; the reality that this person with whom you Conceive depends on and benefits from your best efforts. It is this very pressure that keeps you in tip-top shape, focusing on your Work Positive Dream Team and filtering out the negative. Collaborate with accountability and you Achieve a Work Positive shape that guides your culture to align with your core values, priorities, and unique contribution. Remove the pressure of the relationship, you step back into that negative line of Eeyore Vampires who dominate the work world and compare and compete.

The Golden Rule

The fifth and final characteristic to recognize and build collaborative relationships in Work Positive Dream Teams is they work from the Golden Rule. They treat others the way they want to be treated. They are humble listeners who work for mutual benefit and keep you accountable. The Golden Rule is the foundation of collaborative, Work Positive Dream Team relationships upon which the Conceive core practice is built.

You can name numerous people with whom you enjoy a Golden Rule relationship. You can also think of some persons who possess anything except these characteristics. You might have even spent a few minutes wondering why they are the way they are.

Perhaps these are more than just Eeyore Vampires to you. Maybe you think of them as your enemies. Remember—what you resist, persists. So, simply telling yourself, "I shouldn't be thinking about 'insert name here'" causes your mind to focus on this enemy even more.

Look at your enemies differently. What if you are grateful for them?

Sound crazy? At least counterintuitive, right?

Think about it for a minute. What if instead of demonizing them, you interpret your experiences with them as opportunities to bring out the best in you?

How? You tend to dislike in others what you dislike about yourself.

Read that again: You tend to dislike in others what you dislike about yourself.

So, if one of your enemies has a certain core value or priority that really bothers you, ask yourself, "Why is that?"

Could it be that you see your own core value or priority and the way you work out of it reflected back? Or that you struggle with the temptation to work that way and dislike that about yourself?

Redefine reality around your enemies. Sure, you may lack a collaborative, Work Positive Dream Team relationship with this Eeyore Vampire. And yet what have you really done if you return negativity for negativity? Simply multiplied the Gross Negative Product at work and sent out more negative vibrations that attracts more negative customers and clients, managers and teammates whom you classify as enemies. You create a Work Negative culture.

Instead, see this person's negative behavior as the opposite of how you work. Use it to keep yourself accountable. Let it bring out the best in you, making you more intentional about collaborative relationships within your Work Positive Dream Team.

Look back on your previous work experiences and ask, "Who are the people who invested in my development?"

Thank them. Celebrate them.

Look around at your current work teams and ask, "Who are the people currently investing in my development?"

Thank them. Celebrate them.

Now look forward into the future of your team and ask, "Who's development do I choose to invest in? How do I coach them to Work Positive on a Dream Team?"

As you look back, around, and ahead, you build your Work Positive Dream Team of collaborators to implement the Conceive core practice. They are humble listeners who work for mutual benefit and keep one another accountable in golden ways.

These people Conceive a Work Positive Dream Team culture and help you do the same.

Grab & Go

Make sure as you begin to "Collaborate with Others" that you:

1. Review your best work shots daily with a Work Positive Dream Team member.
2. Grow your work's flowers toward the persons who bring out the best in you and your work, with whom you share core values and priorities, and who encourage your unique contribution.
3. Choose to ask for help to move your work's big rocks.
4. Collaborate at work with someone who listens and asks you questions.
5. Be humble enough to work on your company's pit crew.
6. Find someone who keeps the pressure on your team's rubber band to fit the positive shape of your company.
7. The Golden Rule works. Work the Golden Rule.

Core Practice 3:

BELIEVE the POSITIVE at Work

chapter 9

You Can Believe the Positive at Work

"I have learned that if one advances confidently in the direction of his dreams, and endeavors to live the life he has imagined, he will meet with a success unexpected in common hours."
—Henry David Thoreau

It was one of those snows you remember for a long time, at least when you live at the beach. It was a large enough snow to make a huge snowman. My wife, older daughter who was almost 3 years old, and I did just that—rolling and piling snow into this 6-foot snowperson. We gave our creation ginger snap eyes, a carrot nose, stick arms, and chocolate chip cookie buttons. My daughter insisted we put a hat on him. And, of course, we named him Frosty.

You see, it was around Christmas and while we watched the snow fall, I read her the story of Frosty and how he came to life one day. So, we had to name him Frosty.

After we finished our Frosty, we stood back and admired him. As we did, she asked, "Daddy, when is he gonna come alive?" She remembered the story.

"I don't know, honey. We'll have to watch and wait," I said.

How do you tell your daughter who believes in the magic of an old silk hat that it's not real? That the story is just a fairy tale written to entertain children?

The next day brought the same question: "Daddy, when is he gonna come alive?"

"I don't know, honey. We'll have to watch and wait," I said. I knew my answer would not satisfy her the next day, but what else could I say?

When the next day came, it brought the same question as before, "Daddy, when is he gonna come alive?"

All I could think of was a miserable, "I don't know, honey."

She was ready with an answer.

"I know, Daddy. He comes alive when we're not looking!"

Ever have a work experience when a project, contract, or opportunity came alive when you weren't looking?

There is more to work than you think there is. What you think exists is based on how you Perceive reality, i.e., what you focus on. Also, it is based on your experiences with others to Conceive. Regardless of how well you collaborate with positive people, there is still something that escapes you.

Work comes alive when you aren't looking.

You hold certain beliefs about work; about your teammates and supervisor, customers and clients, about your ability to provide for your family, and still other beliefs. You emotionally invest these beliefs in your work. There is still much about your work that redefines reality as accurate as your beliefs might be. Your work comes alive from time to time when you're not looking.

This redefinition of your reality makes it possible for you to Work Positive in a way that defies description in a spreadsheet. Otherwise work is confined to the prison of what you think about and experience with others. Unfortunately, that is negative for so many people.

You Perceive and Conceive a Work Positive culture, and you Believe your work can come alive when you're not looking; that there are resources beyond your immediate control that converge in miraculous ways for your success and of those around you.

You now know how to Perceive, focusing on the positive while avoiding just the "familiar," and then filtering out your negative thoughts. That's the first core practice. The second core practice is to Conceive by cooperating with and surrounding yourself with positive people with whom you collaborate rather than compare and compete. The third core practice, Believe, is how you redefine your reality and imagine that your work can exceed your expectations, despite this negative world. This third core practice is the emotional dynamic of how you create a Work Positive culture that increases productivity and profits.

chapter 10

Believe Your Birthright

You'll see it when you believe it.
—Wayne Dyer

D id you hear about the man who took his first airplane ride? He didn't really want to go, but was finally persuaded to try it. Scared to death, he got in the plane. The pilot took off, circled the field and landed safely. Someone asked him, "Well, now that wasn't so bad, was it?"

And the man said, "I'll tell you this much. I never did put my full weight down in that thing!"

Do You Trust the Unfamiliar?

I can relate with that guy. Oftentimes I don't trust something new. Other times, I'm just afraid of trying it.

Why? I limit how I Perceive and Conceive my work to my five senses--only the things I can see, hear, taste, touch, and smell. And yet my senses are not always accurate. There is a realm of reality beyond my own senses. Your work experience is like mine, right?

For instance, the company forecasts sales and revenue. If you Work Positive in a retail environment, you analyze a great deal of data like web and foot traffic counts and patterns, demographic information within a certain geographic proximity to your location, and psychographic profiles of your ideal customer. Then you determine a percentage of these figures, based on other research you did regarding industry standards, projecting how many customers will spend what amount of money within a certain time frame. In doing so, you create a year one, two, and three sales forecast. You believe this retail operation will do this amount of business based on the best information you can find. You plan your work accordingly.

A different reality emerges through year one, two, and three. Your work comes alive when you're not looking some quarters. You exceed your forecast. In other quarters, you come close, and miss your marks. Other quarters are way off.

This reality lies beyond your five senses. While you can expect the unexpected, it's virtually impossible to predict based on what you know today. Work is rarely what you think it is.

For example, a couple of sisters walked into a Goodwill store in Danville, Virginia. They were mostly browsing, just slightly interested in anything, and more interested in the shopping experience. One sister found an attractive pearl necklace. She liked it, tried it on, and decided to buy it for sixty-nine cents.

She returned home to Arizona where she wore the pearls, and someone complimented her. She told her story to which the person responds, "Oh, I think they're worth more than 69 cents. You should have those appraised."

She did. The pearl necklace was valued at $50,000.

Your definition of reality misses the mark sometimes. You put your full weight down without even knowing it.

Do you think the donor of that necklace to Goodwill would like that one back? Or, that Goodwill wishes it knew then what it knows now? Reality gets redefined quickly. Resources beyond your ability to influence, control, or manipulate converge in unexplainable ways.

Here's another example. A man was walking through a gem and mineral show when he saw a potato-sized rock. It was not attractive at all, rather garish, in fact, particularly when compared to all the other beautiful stones. The price tag read twenty dollars.

"You want twenty dollars for this?" the man asked the vendor.

The vendor said, "Well, yeah, but you can have it for ten dollars."

The ten-dollar potato-sized rock turned out to be a star sapphire weighing more than 1,000 carats and worth more than one million dollars.

Again, your definition of reality misses the mark. You put your full weight down without even knowing it.

Do you think the vendor of that "rock" wanted a "do-over" on that one? Reality gets redefined quickly.

You define work based on the best information and interpretation of your experiences that you know in the moment. You pretty much only know what you see, the outward appearance of the situation that's evident. And yet, there is a reality beyond the apparent.

Your work comes alive when you're not looking. So, you Believe in the positive and fuel your work with optimism about possibilities you have yet to envision.

My Grandmother Faucette gave my brother and me a chocolate bunny every spring when I was a kid. I always looked forward to getting it, but there were some chocolate bunnies I liked better than others. I never really knew which chocolate bunny I had received until I bit into it because they all looked alike.

Some years when I bit into the bunny, there was nothing but air inside. She gave us a hollow chocolate bunny.

Other years, I bit into the chocolate bunny which looked like the hollow bunnies and discovered that she gave us a marshmallow-filled one. It was great because at least it had something inside.

My favorite years were those when I bit into the chocolate bunny that looked exactly like the hollow and marshmallow-filled ones and found that our grandmother gave us a solid chocolate bunny; chocolate all the way through.

We discovered which kind of bunny we received as we bit into it.

Your work reality gets redefined bite by bite. What appears to be apparent changes.

You Are Born to Believe

There is so much at work that you simply misunderstand. There is much more to team relations, customer satisfaction, and vendor contracts than you can see. hear, taste, touch, and smell.

We are born to Believe that reality defies description and experience. You have had many similar experiences in which your work came alive when you weren't looking. Resources converged in miraculous ways that you just didn't anticipate.

Over the years, I spoke to and coached numerous insurance agents in how to create a Work Positive culture. When I talked with them about this third core practice—Believe—I asked them to remember an occasion when they made a presentation that seemed to go nowhere. They lacked positive traction or reaction at all from the client. Perhaps the response was the deadly phrase, "I want to think about it." They left the appointment saying, "Well, I'll never hear from that person again."

A few days, or weeks, or months later, the agent gets a call from that same client saying something like, "I know you recommended I buy $250,000 of term life insurance, but I think I want to go with the $1,000,000 universal policy instead. Is that OK with you?" Of course, the agent says, "Yes!" and once again experiences how quickly reality redefines for us when unexpected resources converge.

Your version of work reality is less than what is available to you. Remember the daylilies and birds and how they inexplicably trust a universal abundance? Resources converge that are beyond your ability to control much less manipulate and even at times influence.

Consider How You Work Positive . . .

Relive an experience you had in which, like the insurance agent, you observed resources beyond your control converging most wonderfully, contrary to what you expected to happen. How was this experience an example of how you are born to Believe? Scan here to share online with the Work Positive Community

#culturecounts

I loved playing baseball when I was a little boy. I played third base for the Little League White Sox team. Brooks Robinson was my third-base idol. My plans were for him to play for the Orioles until I grew up and came to take his place at the "hot box."

I batted "cleanup" in our lineup. Henry Aaron was my hero. He made the ball fly out of any park on any given day. I dreamed of meeting him one day.

I remember one great game I had at the plate with several base hits, driving in some runs. I came to bat with two outs, runners on base. Visions of "Hammerin' Hank" ran through my mind.

The other team changed pitchers, putting in their best one—a big guy with a fastball that sizzled as it popped into the catcher's mitt.

I stepped into the batter's box, ready to get a base hit. But after three pitches, the umpire screamed, "Strike three, you're out!"

I couldn't believe it. I struck out.

I walked back to the dugout, my eyes filling with tears of disappointment. My coach, Ed Shackleford, met me halfway with the words, "It's all right, Joey. You'll get 'em next time."

I was so disappointed I refused to believe there would be a "next time." I believed that this particular at-bat was it. My coach redefined my reality. He believed that there would be a next time. I only saw my failure in the moment. He believed that there would be a next time, and I would get a hit. I didn't think I would ever hit the ball again.

I eventually believed, too. Coach Shackleford was right. I finished the season batting around .500.

Believing is a challenge for we mature, sophisticated adults. Your mind craves the familiar with its neural pathways and folders ready to receive similar information. Remember the old dog and new tricks? How the hardest part is unlearning the old tricks?

As a child, you constantly carved out neural pathways. From your birth, you imprinted people and experiences with a certain sense of awe and wonder over the many faces of reality.

New experiences thrilled you because you were fascinated with everything. You absorbed it all like a sponge.

You must reclaim your birthright to Believe so you create a Work Positive culture. You are born to believe. As a child you Believed that life is more about what you have yet to experience than it is about what you do. It is only as an adult you began to define your reality as what you can influence, control, and manipulate. Those same mental folders labeled "Familiar" shaped and formed your version of reality.

You Believe only in what you know to be true.

Your beliefs about reality determine how well you work. What you Believe about how you can work with excellence, combined with how you Perceive and Conceive it, charts your culture success.

The good news is that the reality from which you Work Positive is far greater than you can understand. Your perception is finite. Your relationships are limited. You can suspend your disbelief to at least acknowledge that the borders of your current reality are pretty close in. You put your full weight down in this reality. It devalues some things worth much more like pearl necklaces and potato-sized rocks. "Dead" experiences come back to life in a reality you once saw as impossible. There is far more to your Work Positive culture than you imagine now.

What you Believe about your work can come true.

You understood this truth as a child. You trusted this ultimate reality that you saw only in a glimpse, that you heard only in a whisper, that you could only taste in a sip, that you could only touch lightly like a feather, that you could only smell in a whiff.

You can Believe in this ultimate work-reality again, even if just to acknowledge that it only comes alive when you aren't looking. You can trust that you are born to Believe in more resources than you can control, manipulate, or influence. You can grow in that direction.

How Does Your Work-Belief Grow?

I was working out on our farm one beautiful afternoon, clearing small trees and brush away from our electric fence line. I worked along a section of fence and noticed three saplings growing together. The farthest sapling was under the shade of a more mature tree, so it received less light. That sapling changed its growth pattern because of the mature tree. It grew at a forty-five-degree angle up through its companion saplings. It grew toward the light, changing its normal way of growing straight up. It grew taller and fuller than the others because it adapted.

This sapling grew into the light, adapting to the best, available light, doing what it was born to do. If a sapling can adapt and overcome, you can, too.

You were born to Believe you can grow toward the light of a Work Positive culture, turning away from what you only see, hear, taste, touch and smell.

Consider How You Work Positive . . .

. . . and consider what positive light is shining on your work right now. How can you choose to grow toward that positive light? Scan here to share online with the Work Positive Community

#culturecounts

Help to Pull the Load

When you deny your birthright to Believe, you isolate yourself from the converging of infinite resources in unexplainable ways. You bear the weight of working alone, taking on so many responsibilities that you devolve from "human being" to "human doing." You push on a problem teammate, kick on the chaos of chronic interruptions, and deny that a customer could ever be dissatisfied with your work. You fail to budge any of them regardless of your efforts. You sit down and quit, refusing to engage emotionally with your work and discover new solutions.

There is a better way to Believe.

The story is told of a man driving a wagon pulled by a mule named Jim. When everyone got on the wagon, the driver yelled, "Giddyup, Jim. Giddyup, Sue. Giddyup, Sam. Giddyup, John. Giddyup, Joe."

As the wagon started to move, a passenger wondered why the wagon master called all those names and said, "Why do you call the other names when Jim is the one and only mule you have there?"

And the owner said, "If Jim knew he was the only one pulling this wagon, he wouldn't budge an inch."

You really don't know what you can do at work until you claim your birthright to Believe that like Jim, you are yoked with a team of infinite resources that pull alongside you. You Perceive, Conceive, and Believe to create a lot more horsepower for dealing with work challenges than you imagine. Believe and you emotionally engage your work at a previously unexplored level of success. Believe and the impossible becomes possible.

You were born to Believe in an ultimate reality far larger than what you know now.

There is far more to your Work Positive culture of increasing productivity and profits than you now imagine.

You were born to Believe that there is more available in your work to produce the kind of lifestyle you want for yourself and your family. Every day you must claim this birthright if you want to Work Positive, because the negative world will deny your birthright.

You grow away from the positive light of unlimited, converging resources and toward the darkness of your own ego when you turn away from your birthright to Believe.

Grab & Go

Claim these positive thoughts as you "Believe Your Birthright":

1. Your work-reality gets redefined quickly as resources you didn't see coming converge.
2. Believe you work for a solid-chocolate bunny corporation.
3. There is always a next time at bat at work.
4. Your customers and clients, teammates and leaders bring far more valuable resources than you might imagine.
5. Believe you are yoked with a team of infinite resources that pull along with you.
6. Discover and grow toward the light of the positive in your work.
7. You were born to Believe that your work will exceed your expectations.

chapter 11

Bend Away from Ego

"Success is never final; failure is never fatal.
It's courage that counts."
—Winston Churchill

E ver get so overwhelmed by work that you get anxious? Tempted to quit trying? Afraid of failing?

Does It Feel Like the First Time?

Sure, you do. And more than once.

You failed the first time you tried to walk. Your epic steps lasted nanoseconds and then you fell down. Thankfully, you wore a diaper to buffer your bottom. You got up and kept trying until you stayed up on your wobbly legs. You chose to get up when you fell.

You walk today.

And I'll bet you almost drowned the first time you tried to swim. You stayed in the water until you learned to trust it to support you. Today you swim.

Did you hit or kick a ball the first time you swung at it? Nope, but you stayed after it until you made contact. You can hit or kick a ball today.

What about riding a bike? Remember skinning your knees and elbows, crying while your parent cleaned you up? Yet you can ride a bike today.

You were courageous in the face of repeated failures.

Your natural response may be to give up, to find something you're good at and do only that rather than risk humiliation and embarrassment. Staying in this lane means you influence, control, and manipulate those actions and people around you to conform to your standards of behavior—your perfect reality. Perfect because you're in charge.

You choose to exercise your ego rather than Believe. You engage your narcissism because of the negative work culture. You bend inward towards your ego.

Warning Sign: Dead-End Ahead

The dead-end road to your assumed perfection is paved with thoughts like this:

"When I influence, control, and manipulate my customers and everyone else, I am successful. My work runs according to my schedule. I accomplish my goals in my time. I have everything I want. I work harder, am more brilliant and do more than anyone. I am self-made."

Consider How You Work Positive . . .

What or who are you trying to influence, control, and manipulate? So, how's this logic working for you? Scan here to share online with the Work Positive Community

#culturecounts

The self-made teammate works negative, restricted by ego limitations, pursuing an assumed perfection.

Avoid such self-made Eeyore Vampires as if they have a deadly, communicable disease.

They do.

Sometimes avoiding them is impossible. Sometimes you are one.

Have You Met Yourself Lately?

That's right. Sometimes you allow the negative noise of work to crowd out the positive melody of purpose and passion you long to hear. It's so easy to stop up your ears, hum to yourself, and believe the lie. Drowning out the present noise is a challenge.

One cold winter's night, I was sitting in my favorite recliner at home, trying to have a conversation with my wife. She was seated in the chair next to me with only a lamp table between us. I realized that I was yelling to be heard. So, I listened around the room for a moment and discovered why. First, the TV was on, blaring through our speaker system. It had to be on loud enough to be heard over the fan that blew hot air from the gas logs. Because the gas logs were on and dry out the air, we ran a humidifier with its fan blowing. Throw in a couple of daughters talking, and it's no wonder I yelled.

So, I got up out of my recliner and turned off the humidifier, turned back the fan blowing hot air from the gas logs, turned down the TV, and said, "Shhh" to our daughters. Then I sat back down, smiled at my wife, and said, "There, that's better." We heard each other without yelling.

Does the negative noise of work prevent you from hearing the positive? It is so easy to disbelieve that resources converge without your direct intervention. That's when you bend your work in toward your ego. Think of it as economic navel gazing.

You self-consume. The insatiable emotional appetite of your ego black-holes everything positive, spewing only negative noises. These noises interfere with the Work Positive culture. These noises sound like:

Fears about finances—"Sales are down. What if there's a lay-off?"

Suspicions about a teammate—"He sure talks about our competition a lot. Could he be feeding them information?"

Mistrust of a vendor—"She says she's doing us a special favor with this contract, but I wonder if she's telling the truth."

These noisy worries and more assault your ability to Work Positive. You bend further inward toward your ego, determined to pull yourself up by your own bootstraps.

Work Will Be Better When . . .

So, you go to work with negative noise booming through your ego. You say to yourself, "I'll be OK. Work will be better when . . .

I get some new teammates."

I move up to a new position."

I find a new job with a better company."

I . . ."

Sure, you're important at work. However, your work is more than the sum total of you.

It just seems that way when the economic noise assaults you at incredibly difficult decibel levels and your first recourse is to bend in to your ego. You then set up unrealistic "perfect stages" of your work when everything will be just right.

Your ego fears failure, rejection, and a host of other paralyzing scenarios, none of which exist except in your emotions. Your brain is unable to distinguish between this imaginary fear and reality. Such fear prevents you from getting up and doing what you can.

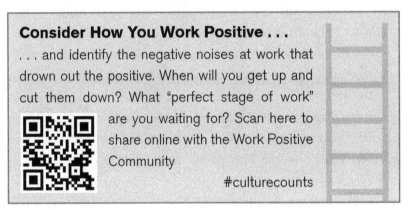

Consider How You Work Positive . . .

. . . and identify the negative noises at work that drown out the positive. When will you get up and cut them down? What "perfect stage of work" are you waiting for? Scan here to share online with the Work Positive Community

#culturecounts

It's a Sweet and Sour Life

The reality is from the moment you accepted your first job until now you experienced challenges. What you believe about these challenges determines your work-reality and whether you Achieve your work dreams.

Are these challenges the worst of times? Or, are they the best of times?

My wife prepared sweet and sour chicken for supper one evening. I watched as our older daughter ate her third piece and said to her, "You really like sweet and sour chicken, don't you?"

"Yes, sir!" she said. "But I like the sweet part best. I told Mama I just wanted the sweet, not the sour part of the sauce."

I gave my wife the "And what did you say?" look. She smiled and said, "I explained that the sweet and the sour were together in the sauce and that I couldn't separate them."

"That's OK," our daughter said as she ate that third piece, "I still like the sweet part best."

I'm like our daughter. I like just the sweet part of work. No sour experiences! Nothing like an Eeyore Vampire teammate to make my tongue curl or my mouth pucker up. No jerk for a boss who causes my eyes to water. No demanding, unreasonable customer to churn my stomach acid.

You want everything to go your way. As it is with sauce, so it is with work. The sweet and the sour are together.

The way you Work Positive is more about what you Believe to be reality than you ever imagined. Maybe that's why you picked up this book about how to *Work Positive in a Negative World: Team Edition*. You know the sour parts, the negativity of work today. You exercised your ego to the point of exhaustion, trying to make something perfect out of your problems, or to at least get some forward momentum. You're hoping there is more to work than what you and your ego have done so far.

The good news is that there is much more to work today than you imagine. Remember that moment when you accepted your current position? Hope for success peeks up through the cold adversity of your ego-constructed work like the first crocus of spring through six inches of snow.

You were born to Believe that you can create a Work Positive culture that increases productivity and profits. You can avoid bending inward to your ego.

You are actually at your best when you work from your birthright to Believe and imagine how you best Work Positive. Let's discover how now.

Grab & Go

Remember these as you work to "Bend Away from Ego":

1. You fell down more than you walked when you were first learning to walk. Yet you walk today. Keep believing.
2. Avoid self-made Eeyore Vampires as if they have a deadly, communicable disease. They do. Unfortunately, you can't always avoid them. Sometimes you are one.
3. Noisy worries assault your desire to Work Positive.
4. Your work is always filled with challenges. Choose to build on the sweet parts while acknowledging the sour.
5. You were born to Believe instead of bend inward to your ego.
6. Hope for your work success peeks up through the cold adversity of your ego-constructed work like the first crocus of spring through six inches of snow.
7. You are actually at your best when you work from your birthright to Believe and imagine how you can Work Positive in a negative world.

Best to Imagine

"We have a positive vision of the future founded on the belief that the gap between the promise and reality of America can one day be finally closed. We believe that."
—Barbara Jordan

A friend of mine traveled through Ireland with a tour group. They drove by bus through the beautiful countryside, admiring the rolling hills and green pastures.

My friend noticed that trees bordered the road. The more she looked at them the more she realized that they were all planted and grown the exact distance apart. She asked her tour guide about the trees.

"Oh, yes," the tour guide told her. "Those trees were originally fence posts cut locally from trees. They were planted exactly five feet apart as fence posts. The soil is so rich here that the planted fence posts started sprouting limbs and eventually grew into trees again."

Consider How You Work Positive . . .

. . . and honestly answer this question: Would you have imagined that fence posts can grow into trees again? Why? Scan here to share online with the Work Positive Community

#culturecounts

Are You Settling for Less Than?

You forfeit your created capacity to Believe when you bend your work inward toward your ego. You define your work practices as only those things and people that you can influence, control, and manipulate when your corporate policy is narcissism. Ego prompts you to give away the keys to imagine your work culture as positive.

As you discovered in the Perceive core practice, your mind is content without imagining. Your brain abhors the unfamiliar. You are mentally satisfied with the familiar. It is OK with your mind to only imagine your work as what it is right now. Ignorance is bliss, right?

How well do you avoid the unfamiliar at work? The context in which you work changes every single day. You bend inward toward your ego as you cater to your mind's laziness and refuse to accept these unfamiliar changes. You settle for less than you can Achieve. You stop short of fulfilling your dreams. And the day will come when you say, "I wish I had known and done something about it."

Our younger daughter had an experience like this. She is introverted and prefers to avoid a crowd. It was a big deal when she sang in the elementary school chorus at a Parents-Teachers Organization (PTO) meeting of several hundred people.

Of course, she did great, knowing all the lyrics and following her director closely. Afterwards, as we drove home and talked, she was so relieved that the whole thing was over.

"How did you feel?" I asked her.

"My stomach felt funny when I was up on the stage," she said.

I told her, "Oh, those were butterflies."

"How did butterflies get in my stomach?" she asked.

"They weren't really butterflies," I explained. "It just felt like butterflies flying around your stomach."

"Well," she said, "I wish I had known they were butterflies because I would have opened my mouth and let them out."

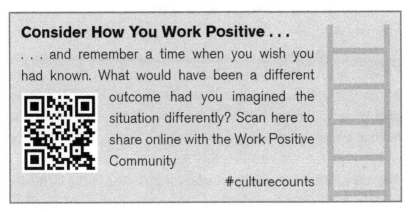

Consider How You Work Positive . . .

. . . and remember a time when you wish you had known. What would have been a different outcome had you imagined the situation differently? Scan here to share online with the Work Positive Community

#culturecounts

See How It Works?

If you only knew then what you know now: you were born to Believe rather than bend inward toward your ego.

There is one you among billions of people which means you can Work Positive and imagine you at your best. Imagination is your pilot through the Skies of Unfamiliar. It is the jet fuel of how you create a Work Positive culture that attracts top talent and reduces team turnover. It propels you off the runway of the negative world and takes you into the stratosphere of where you

Believe that all things are possible. The tail wind of resources converges behind you and sends you soaring.

Imagine it like this: You focus your thoughts on the positive strengths of your work, accept the unfamiliar changes, and filter out the negative possibilities. You Perceive.

You cooperate with a team of positive persons whom you attract, compare and compete rarely, and collaborate quite well. You Conceive.

Then Team (enter your name here) Positive—customers and clients, leaders and teammates, vendors and suppliers alike—Believe together that the organization can grow in phenomenal ways, and imagine a broader range of positive solutions you can offer and Achieve.

See how it works?

Imagination is the emotional key to creating a Work Positive culture. You Perceive, Conceive, and Believe based on more than what you alone can see, hear, taste, touch, and smell, and include what you can imagine. You engage your work emotionally with purpose and passion. The impossible becomes possible. The unexpected happens. Top talent is attracted. Team turnover reduces. A Work Positive culture increases productivity and profits.

The company's success is the culmination of how you think about it, partner with others to think about it, and then collectively imagine outcomes that seem unrealistic at the moment, and yet are achievable as all of you Believe.

You've picked up an acorn before and looked at it. It is about the size of a dime. Most likely you picked it up under an oak tree. Recently, I picked up an acorn under one of our oak trees that's at least 150 years old. I stood there looking at the acorn, looking up at the tremendous oak, while wondering, "How did such a huge tree start as such a little acorn?" It defies my senses to understand or explain. I can only imagine.

Have you ever held a mustard seed in the palm of your hand? It's about the size of a pencil point. You plant that pencil-point seed and it grows into a six-foot-high bush. Who would have thought that was possible? You Work Positive as you Believe that all the imagination you need to do the impossible is about the size of that mustard seed.

I remember watching my Great-Grandmother Frazier make yeast rolls. In fact, I have the bread bowl that she and her daughter, my Grandmother Greene, used to mix flour and milk. She sifted the flour, and added the liquid and other ingredients. Then she opened a very small packet of something magical called yeast. She dropped just a pinch or so in, an extremely small amount when compared with the flour. Next she mixed it all. Grabbing a handful of it, she patted it out and put it down on the pan and let it sit.

I remember asking her, "Grandma, what's it doing?"

"It's rising, son," she said.

And I asked, "How?"

"The yeast makes it rise," she told me.

And I remember wondering, "How in the world does such a tiny amount of yeast make all that dough rise?"

Your imagination is like yeast. You rise to Achieve when you Work Positive and Believe that your work will succeed in ways that defy your ability to logically understand.

I remember planting corn with my Grandfather Greene. He involved me at every step of the process. We opened fifty-pound bags of corn seed and poured them into the planter mounted on the tractor. I dug my hand into the open sack, and stirred up the seed, pulling out a handful.

"Granddaddy," I said, "How can these little seeds fill this whole field with corn?"

He replied, "Son, this tiny corn seed becomes a huge corn stalk that produces more ears that contain more seeds that grow more stalks."

"But how does it do it?" I insisted.

"I don't know," he said. "I just know these seeds grow every time I plant them."

You Work Positive when you imagine more than you Perceive with your five-senses. Sometimes you just have to Believe that if the impossible happened once, it will happen again . . . even if it first happened for someone else.

One of my favorite TV programs growing up was "The Beverly Hillbillies." Jed Clampett was a backwoods sort of guy, living humbly in a run-down shack. He was hunting one day, shot at his prey and missed, but "up through the ground came a-bubblin' crude . . . oil, that is . . . black gold . . . Texas tea . . . ." Jed stumbled on a huge well of oil.

Now if you're Jed Clampett, do you complain about that greasy slick stuff that gets on your boots and keeps your crops from growing? Or, do you buy up all the land in the adjacent area and phone ExxonMobil?

You Work Positive as your imagination bubbles up and you envision new work possibilities, and viable solutions to problems for yourself and others that can be marketed and sold. Why you might even see yourself around a cement pond!

Consider How You Work Positive . . .

. . . and recall a time in your work journey when something seemingly small and insignificant grew into something large and meaningful. Scan here to share online with the Work Positive Community

#culturecounts

An Apple a Day Keeps the Disbelief Away

I hand out apples as I speak to work groups about how to create a Work Positive culture. I ask, "How many apples are you holding?"

Of course, the first answer I get is "One" and usually the person says, "Hey, that wasn't so hard."

"OK, one," I say. Anyone have another answer?"

The room gets quiet and then, usually from the back of the room, I hear someone say, "A bushel."

And I ask, "How so?"

This person usually says, "Well, you can plant the seeds in this apple and grow a bushel of other apples."

And then I ask, "Just a bushel?"

Someone else answers, "No, you can get an orchard out of this apple."

"An orchard?" I say.

And then someone else says, "Oh, more than an orchard. There's an infinite number of apples in this apple."

"How's that?" I ask.

"You plant these seeds and they produce an orchard of apples. And from the seeds of those apples, you grow other orchards and those orchards grow still more orchards and pretty soon you can't count all the orchards."

You Work Positive when you Believe that you hold in your hand everything required to create a Work Positive culture of increasing productivity and profits. When bent to ego, you hold only what you see, hear, taste, touch, and smell—what you can influence, control, and manipulate.

Your work holds so much more than that . . . if you Believe that what you Perceive and Conceive in collaborative relationships will produce an infinite harvest.

You plant these culture seeds in your work and water, fertilize, cultivate, and get adequate sun to them as they bravely push up through the soil. And yet do you actually make the seed grow? Or, do you simply provide the conditions for a miracle to happen?

One of my favorite movie series is the Indiana Jones one. It reminds me of the westerns my Dad, brother, and I enjoyed watching on Saturdays.

There is a scene toward the end of one movie in the series that I love. Indiana Jones is pursuing an artifact known as the Holy Grail. It is the cup that Jesus drank from at the Last Supper. Indy has endured every kind of danger known to humanity, but he, his hat, and his bullwhip have made it through to this last test.

He stands on the edge of a bottomless pit. The pit separates him from the Holy Grail, yet he is close enough to see it. His clue indicates that if he believes, the way to the Chalice will appear to him. Everything he sees tells him that he will plunge to his death should he step off the precipice.

Indiana Jones decides that he has come too far not to believe, so he closes his eyes, fully expecting to fall to his death, and yet takes that first step forward. Much to his surprise, a bridge to the other side appears under his feet. An optical illusion prevented him from seeing the bridge until he took that first step. Rather than dying, he runs across, seizes the cup, and returns safely.

The First Step Away Is the Hardest

Just like with Indiana Jones, that first step away from the illusion you see now to what you Believe is the hardest.

You Work Positive when you Believe that tiny acorns become huge oak trees, small mustard seeds become great bushes, pinches of yeast make wonderful rolls, a little corn seed produces bushels of ears, a trivial bubbling up of crude oil is worth buying a farm over, and a single apple has within it an infinite number of apples. You Work Positive when you imagine that the first step you take away from what you see now to what you Believe will literally cause the ground to rise up underneath your feet. This first step is how you redefine your reality and Achieve your dreams. That first step starts the attraction of top talent, the reduction of team turnover, and the creation of a positive work culture that increases productivity and profits.

You Achieve your full potential as you imagine your work at its very best. I've discovered in my coaching practice that the mundane minutia of work can consume most of your time, energy, and attention, leaving none for imagining work at its best.

If you keep doing what you've always done, you'll get what you've always got. How does that move you closer to creating a Work Positive culture?

Then let's take a few minutes to imagine your work Achieves more, accomplishing what might seem impossible now. Most of my clients find this exercise works best with the door shut, the smartphone turned off, and the desk phone on "Do Not Disturb."

In Figure 12.1, three simple yet profound questions guide your imagining.

FIGURE 12.1

1. If I handed you a magic wand to wave, and money were no object, what would your work look like today?

_____

   A. Imagine your teammates. How many are there?

   _____

   What are their core values, priorities, and unique contributions?

   _____

   What do they tell their spouses about working with you?

   _____

   B. Imagine your customers and clients. How many are there?

   _____

   What solutions are you providing them?

   _____

   What do they say to their friends when talking about you and your work?

   _____

   C. Imagine your suppliers and vendors. How many are there?

   _____

   How do they offer to help you Achieve your work dreams?

   _____

   What do they tell their friends about you?

   _____

2. What is your current reality of doing business?

_____

Answer as you best understand the company you work for today.

A. Employees

_____

B. Customers and clients

_____

C. Suppliers and vendors

_____

3. Name three actions you can take in the next 21 days to close the gap between how you imagine your work and your current reality.

Action 1/Week 1:

_____

Action 2/Week 2:

_____

Action 3/Week 3:

_____

What will be different about your work at the end of week 3?

_____

How will it more closely resemble your redefined work reality in item 1?

_____

Grab & Go

Remember that it's "Best to Imagine" how you Work Positive and that:

1. Fence posts grow into trees.
2. Tiny acorns grow sky-high oak trees.
3. Pencil-point mustard seeds grow head-tall bushes.
4. Black gold bubbles up from the hunting grounds of your work.
5. An apple seed grows an infinite number of apples.
6. A pinch of yeast rises a pan of rolls.
7. The ground literally rises up beneath your feet when you keep your eyes on the prize of your Work Positive culture.

Core Practice 4:

ACHIEVE the POSITIVE at Work

chapter 13

You Can Achieve the Positive at Work

I've come to believe that all my past failure and frustration were actually laying the foundation for the understandings that have created the new level of living I now enjoy.
—Tony Robbins

A woman drove down a heavily traveled street one afternoon after getting off work a little early. The radio was blasting her favorite song, when suddenly her car quit. She managed to steer it over to the side of the street. She got out and looked under the hood, not really knowing what she was searching for, but it just seemed the thing to do.

An unfamiliar voice behind her said, "Lady, do you need some help?" She wheeled around to discover three young men standing behind her.

"Uh, no. Everything is fine," she said. "I'm calling AAA. They're on their way."

"You don't need to call anyone," one of the young men said, and grabbed her phone. The next thing she knew, she was on the ground, trying to cover her face and protect herself from the strong-armed blows pummeling her face first, then her stomach. Then kick after kick broke her ribs. She lost consciousness as blood oozed from her lips.

No one saw anything as the three young men managed to start the vehicle and drove away.

About a half-hour later, a highly esteemed and successful businessman was chauffeured in his limo down that same street. His driver slowed down when he spotted the woman lying on the sidewalk. He could see the pool of blood.

"Mr. James, there's a woman bleeding badly on the sidewalk over here. I'm going to get out and check on her," the driver said.

"No, you're not," Mr. James yelled back. "If I'm not at this meeting on time, I'll lose this loan. Drive on . . . now!"

"Can I at least call it in to 9-1-1?" the driver asked.

"Of course not," Mr. James said. "Then we'll have to come back and waste our time giving a statement. Turn left at the next intersection and take a back street to The Continental."

A few minutes later, an ethics professor from the local university stopped at the traffic light near where the woman was on the sidewalk, still bleeding. He peered through his windshield, not sure at first what he was seeing.

"That couldn't be a woman down on the sidewalk, could it?" he wondered. He slowly pulled away from the traffic light and stared at her, noticing the fresh pool of blood.

"It is, and she's bleeding profusely," he said out loud. "I'd better stop," and he slowed down to pull over and then thought better of it.

"Her attackers may still be around and assault me if I get out to help," he decided. He sped away, turning off the street, just in case the criminals were watching.

Just then a construction worker pulled up to the traffic light. His beat-up work truck just barely kept running while waiting for the light to change. He tapped out a back-beat on his steering wheel to his favorite song on the radio.

His glance fell on what looked like someone lying on the sidewalk. Not waiting for the light to change, he checked the intersection, and pulled quickly over to the curb beside where the woman was lying half dead. He jumped out of the truck and ran to her side.

"Hey lady! Are you OK?" he asked.

She only moaned, and tried to cover her face with her arms.

"I don't have a cell phone," he told her. He stood there, then started pacing, trying to figure out what to do.

"Lady," he said, "I'm going to put you in my truck and take you to the hospital, OK?" And with that, he picked up the woman in her blood-stained dress, and gently placed her on the passenger seat in his truck, carefully shutting the door. He ran around to the driver's side, jumped in, and sped off down the street toward Mercy General.

Screeching in on two wheels, he pulled up to the Emergency Department door. He jumped out and ran in and screamed, "Somebody come help. A woman has been attacked."

A man and a woman flew out the door, one of them screaming, "Bring a gurney and prep a room stat." They lifted the woman from the truck, placed her on the stretcher, and wheeled her inside.

The construction worker followed closely behind, but when he tried to follow her through the trauma room doors, a loud voice stopped him: "Sir, I must talk with you first."

He pivoted over to the woman at the desk who said to him, "Sir, you must secure payment for our services before we can treat her. This is a private hospital, not one of the county facilities."

Incredulous, the man said, "I just found her on the street. I don't know her."

"I'm sorry, sir," the woman continued. "Our rules are clear. You either secure payment now or take her somewhere else."

The construction worker straightened himself up and said, "I will gladly pay for your services."

He pulled his wallet out and handed her his medical insurance card, not knowing how he would explain this to his boss, but knowing what he had to do. "And here," he said, handing her his credit card. "Whatever else it costs that my insurance doesn't cover, you can put on my card."

Now which of these three—the businessman, the ethics professor, or the construction worker—would you say makes things happen? Is a person of positive action?

Knowing how to Perceive at work, focusing on the positive and filtering out the negative is the first core practice of your Work Positive culture. The second core practice is to Conceive it, that is, cooperate and collaborate with others as you work. The third core practice is to redefine your work reality and Believe so you emotionally engage with your work, avoid your bent to ego and imagine your work at its very best.

The fourth core practice is about how you Achieve a Work Positive culture that increases productivity and profits; how you act on all of the previous internal work to Perceive, Conceive, and Believe, and then Achieve it. This key is the physical dynamic—what you do to Work Positive.

chapter 14

Pay Attention to What's Important

Working in an office with an array of electronic devices is like trying to get something done at home with half a dozen small children around. The calls for attention are constant.
—Marilyn vos Savant

I listened carefully when our younger daughter came home from second grade one day all excited about a science experiment.

"Daddy, it was so cool," she said. "Did you know that a magnet can pick up a nail through a glass jar?"

"Really?" I said.

"It sure can. The magnet picks up the nail through the side of the jar, but it won't pick up the jar," she said.

"Now why is that?" I said.

"Because the nail is attracted to the magnet and the glass isn't."

"What do you mean 'attracted'?" I said.

"That means the nail wants to come to the magnet and the glass doesn't," she explained. "That's why the magnet can pick up the nail."

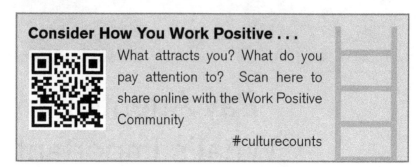

Consider How You Work Positive . . .

What attracts you? What do you pay attention to? Scan here to share online with the Work Positive Community

#culturecounts

A whole new world opened up for her in that one simple classroom experience. She discovered the attraction factor—a universal principle among physical objects and people.

The Attractions at Work are Many

At what point do attractions—physical things to which you give your attention—become distractions?

I have observed over the years of coaching that when a child— let's call him "Johnny"—cannot seem to sit still in his school desk and focus, we run him through a battery of tests, label him "ADD" or "ADHD" or some other alphabet soup name, and medicate him.

When Johnny graduates and grows up, sitting still in his desk long enough to finish an MBA, we stick him in an office somewhere and encourage him to multitask. That means he can't sit still at his desk and focus on one assignment at a time. Everything is now important to Johnny.

So, while he conferences with Asia, he answers an e-mail from a customer in Florida, sends a text to a vendor in Texas, completes a spreadsheet to upload and present at the conference, and his wife is on hold, wondering if he will make it to his seven-year-old daughter's dance recital. We even reward Johnny financially when he is better than anyone else at multitasking all of these "important" tasks. So, we give Johnny a raise as an adult for what we medicated him for in elementary school.

Is this how Johnny Works Positive?

Recent studies indicate that personal productivity diminishes as you multitask and divide your attention between too many sources. You get less done when you try to do more all at once.

You might can do everything, but not all at once.

But Then You Knew That . . .

You choose to Work Positive so you focus and filter for positive thoughts, which means you pay attention to what is important. You prioritize based on certain metrics. That's how you begin to achieve a Work Positive culture of increasing productivity and profits despite the distractions. The only way for you to Achieve what others consider impossible, is to pay attention to your priorities.

File that one under "Easier said than done," right?

Your productivity priorities follow the 80/20 rule—about twenty percent of what you pay attention to and act on contributes eighty percent to your task accomplishment, company revenue, and other metrics. So, who sets your priorities? You based on where you create the most ROI in all kinds of metrics? Or others who set your agenda based on what they think is important or don't want to do?

Technology drives others' choices careening on steroids onto your devices, and all of it is marked "urgent." To Work Positive and Achieve your dreams requires you pay attention to what is most important among your priorities.

Naming those priorities is job one because it focuses your attention on one target at a time.

I'm reminded of my first few quail hunting experiences. I got excited when a large covey of birds flew up. I remember thinking, "Wow! With that many birds flying, I can't miss!" I shot into the covey without really aiming at any bird in particular. I missed every time.

Later, I learned to select one bird, focus my aim on that one bird in the covey, follow it with my gun, and shoot just at that one bird. My accuracy improved greatly. I picked a target, aimed at it, and hit it.

What work activity is your target? How's your aim? Scattered or focused? The results reflect your accuracy to ready, aim, fire.

Life is Busy Today

There are perpetual coveys of work tasks flying in your face all at once daily.

Despite the fact that you have fast food, K-cup coffee and DoorDash, how often do you complete your to-do list?

How do you get ready and focus on one priority task—the most important—take aim, and fire away with your attention and Achieve through aligned action?

My Grandfather Greene told me stories of his childhood when he got up at 4:30 AM to bring in the wood he split previously, put it in the "cook stove," and lit the fire so his mother could prepare breakfast. The most important meal of the day required someone to gather eggs in the dark laid by the hens in the chicken coop. A family member prepared the pig the previous fall for bacon or sausage. The flour ground from their corn was in a sack, ready to make the biscuits with fresh milk from their cows. About the only thing that came from the "dry goods store" was the coffee and salt.

They had a lot to do every morning. The necessary tasks for eating breakfast were understood and done.

Your biggest morning task is to decide whether to stop by Starbucks or make your favorite breakfast smoothie at home. That leaves you an abundance of time to do other things that are important, right? Right?

So, how is that working out for you?

How do you choose which priority action items to aim at? Just shooting into the covey of "urgent" items others put on your to-do list misses the mark.

As you walk away from that day's work are you shaking your head and asking, "What did I get done today?"

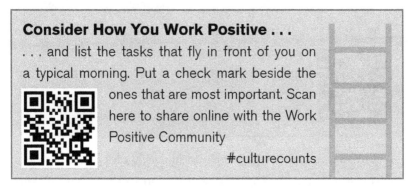

Consider How You Work Positive . . .

. . . and list the tasks that fly in front of you on a typical morning. Put a check mark beside the ones that are most important. Scan here to share online with the Work Positive Community

#culturecounts

What is Important to YOU?

Sometimes what is really important is sacrificed on the altar of what you think is important. Resources converge in a moment and you miss it. You give away your power to choose to someone else and neglect the present moment when you can Achieve positive results.

Those who Achieve do so because they acted in that present moment when resources uniquely converged. Someone would have discovered the light bulb if Thomas Edison had not persevered through more than a thousand ways of not making it. Someone invested in that little startup company when it IPOed, became known around the world as a verb—Google—and now is Alphabet.

Yes, someone acts on what is important and gets outstanding results. They focus on the one priority in the day full of coveys, ready, aim, fire, and hit the mark. They pay attention to what is important because they Perceived it, Conceived it with another, Believed with their imagination, and will Achieve what everyone else considered impossible.

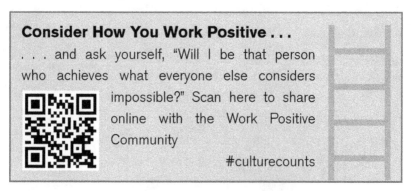

Consider How You Work Positive . . .

. . . and ask yourself, "Will I be that person who achieves what everyone else considers impossible?" Scan here to share online with the Work Positive Community

#culturecounts

As you know, the negative world makes it a lot easier to not be that person. It pushes you to pay attention to the things at work that just are not that important.

When my nephew was seven years old, he and I were watching a football game together. One of the players lost a shoe and had to leave the game.

The player came back on the field and his shoe looked different. My nephew said something about it, and I looked more carefully. The player was in such a hurry to get back on the field that the athletic trainer didn't have time to tape the shoe back on, securing it up his ankle. So, the guy ran back on the field with one shoe taped and the other untaped.

My nephew said, "I thought he had mismatched shoes on," and we laughed about it.

That same player with the different shoes ran the ball on the very next play. He broke several tackles and almost scored. My nephew said, "I guess it doesn't matter whether his shoes match or not if he can run like that."

A negative work culture encourages you to pay attention to the outward appearances like mismatched shoes. Does it really make any difference if your shoes match if you Achieve positive results? When you focus your attention on actions that align with your priorities rather than avoid being different, your work reality redefines. You create a productive Work Positive culture when you pay attention to what's important instead of caving to the multitasking crowd.

What is Your Priority Trigger?

What is your trigger for paying attention to important priorities you choose? What motivates you to give no attention to the mismatched shoes and focus on aligned actions?

I found my trigger some years ago. I had the opportunity to stand by an open grave as a family member was buried. His death was sudden and unexpected. He took his own life. As I stood there, my mind flooded with all the times I wished I had called him just to say, "Hi!"

And then I thought about all the birthday cards I didn't send. The "just because" notes I didn't write. The times I didn't check in with him to see how life was treating him. I cried.

I cried for me. For the lost opportunities while he was here. The words left unsaid. The deeds left undone.

I noticed a dragonfly around that open grave. Dragonflies are such beautiful creatures. Their iridescent wings glitter in the summer sun around ponds, lakes, and wetlands all around the world. Google "dragonflies" and you find literally thousands and thousands of websites about them. There are societies of people that study dragonflies, landscape their yards to attract them, and share what they learn with others. Dragonflies inspire everything from beautiful jewelry to fairy tales.

And yet, most dragonflies live only a month.

So, I stood there at that open grave, staring at dragonflies, and asked myself, "What would I do if I only had a month to live?" I made a decision as I watched the sandy soil fill his grave and cover his casket, dragonflies flitting about: I'm doing better. I now say all the words. I now do rather than wait.

I pay attention to what is important and align my actions. I focus and filter for positive thoughts. I go out of my way to find the unfamiliar. I cooperate and collaborate with other positive people, comparing and competing rarely. I have no Eeyore Vampires on Team Joey. I work from my birthright to Believe and imagine the best in every opportunity that finds me, steering clear of the bent to my ego. My accountability partners sniff out the trail of my ego and redirect me as necessary. I pay attention to what is important, which leads me to Achieve a Work Positive culture.

Care to join me?

Consider How You Work Positive . . .

. . . and reflect on what you would do differently today if you discovered that you had only 30 days to live. Scan here to share online with the Work Positive Community

#culturecounts

Pay Attention to What is Important to You

Here are some proven Work Positive Achieve culture strategies and tactics that coach you in how to pay attention to what is important and align your actions.

Start the Day Quietly

Noise greets from the minute you start work whether at home or an office building. Noise escorts you as you do the end-of-day crawl away from your desk. And noise plays every minute in between. How many moments of quiet do you have to sort out important matters?

Finding a way to start your day quietly is key to achieving a Work Positive culture. A quiet beginning for some in Work Positive Nation means setting technology to "Do Not Disturb." For those working from home, it means getting up before anyone else. For those who commute to an office, it means you lock yourself in the building an hour before you open.

Thirty minutes to an hour seems to be an optimum time period to be quiet. Engage in activities that coach you to sort priorities and focus on the positive. Read a book like this one and complete activities. Meditate on your recent results and welcome unfamiliar thoughts to Conceive with your teammates. Believe as you visualize a stellar work culture.

Your major focus at this time is to silence the noise of work and give yourself the space to Perceive, Conceive, and Believe—all of which propel you to Achieve positive results through aligned actions. That's how you attract top talent and reduce team turnover so you create a positive work culture that increases productivity and profits.

Create Boundaries

The creep of technology intrudes at every step of your work. Learning to Work Positive and pay attention to what is most important translates into daily recognizing the creep and creating boundaries that limit it.

For instance, you're in a meeting. Your desk phone rings. Do you answer it? Do you read the Caller ID window and decide?

Let's say you're working on your computer on an important project. Is your e-mail open? Is it set on "automatic" so that it's making noises and popping up windows that interrupt your flow?

What if you're with a customer and your smartphone buzzes? Do you take it?

I hope your answer is "No" in each case, but I suspect at least sometimes, it's "Yes."

Create boundaries around your technology that allow you to focus completely on what is most important. You pay for technology services. They are to serve you, not vice versa. Turn it off to create space in your workflow.

End Your Day with a Victory

Ever collapse into bed in total exhaustion, convinced that the rats won the race?

Fall asleep in front of the TV, watching the late news as you drift away?

Remember that your mind processes information even while you sleep. Whatever you go to sleep thinking about is what your mind spends the overnight working on.

Negative problems at work invade your dreams.

Negative economic indicators, murders, floods, and other disasters enter your brain for overnight delivery.

Any wonder you're exhausted when you wake up?

Program your mind to pay attention overnight to the important, positive matters of the workday. A new teammate with outstanding credentials. You got more done than you thought possible. A profit and loss statement revealed a nice bump.

Sure, some workdays seem more negative than positive. Wake up refreshed and ready to pay attention to the 20 percent of productive tasks. Focus and filter your thoughts until you reach at least a positive one from the day and pay attention to that as you fall asleep. Re-read the Gratitude Diary section in the Perceive core practice for a specific way to seed positively your sleepy mind.

The Greatest Challenge

Your greatest challenge in paying attention to what is important is doing it rather than just intending to do it. It's easier to intend to pay attention—start each day quietly, create boundaries around technology, and end each day with a victory—than it is to actually do it.

Intention divorced from action is the road to nowhere.

You've been down that road before. What will you do about it now?

Grab & Go

Remember to "Pay Attention to What's Important" and keep in mind that:

1. You get less done when you multitask.
2. You hit nothing when you are unsure of which bird to aim at.
3. The outward appearance of your shoes is insignificant as long as you run well.
4. Go stand before an open grave today. Then decide what's important to you.
5. Start your day quietly.
6. Create boundaries around technology.
7. End your day with victory.

chapter 15

Intention is the Road to Nowhere

"Leaders, whether in the family, in business, in government or in education, must not allow themselves to mistake intentions for accomplishments."
—Jim Rohn

A manager received a call from the cleaning service saying that they could not get someone to the building to clean that week due to a blizzard. All their employees were doing snow removal around the city.

"No problem," the manager said. "We can do it."

So, he called one of his teammates into his office.

"Tom, the cleaning service can't get here this week. So, we're all going to pitch in and do a little cleaning. How about you clean the bathroom? All the supplies are in there."

Tom replied, "Boss, I really don't want to. I clean the toilets at home and I hate it." And he walked out. Later Tom thought more about the manager's request and decided that if he could clean the bathroom at home, he could do it at work. It was not that big a deal. Besides there was no shower at work. So, he did it.

The manager called a second teammate, Ralph, into his office when Tom refused to clean the bathroom. "Ralph, the cleaning service can't get here this week. So, we're all going to pitch in and do a little cleaning. How about you clean the bathroom? All the supplies are in there."

"Sure thing, boss. I'll be glad to," Ralph said. Ralph walked out of the manager's office and never cleaned the bathroom.

Which teammate would you want on your team—Tom or Ralph?

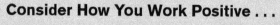

Consider How You Work Positive . . .

When did you say, "No" to someone and then went ahead and did it anyway? And when did you say, "Yes" and decided not to do it? Scan here to share online with the Work Positive Community

#culturecounts

A Story of Two Teammates

Which one, Tom or Ralph, Achieved the positive at work? Which one intended to?

Intentions—"I want to" or "I didn't mean to"—are pathways to achieving positive results, and yet are not the same as achievement. Intention isolated from action doesn't change the outcomes.

Intention, alone, is the road to nowhere.

You can Perceive the positive at work mentally. You can Conceive it with others. You can Believe it and imagine the best possible work results. You can even decide to pay attention to what is most important at work. You fail to Achieve a Work Positive culture of increased productivity when you just intend to act on it.

I talked with a friend that I had not seen in over thirty years. She asked me what I do for fun and I said, "Well, I really enjoy running a mile on a treadmill at the fitness center and working out on the Nautilus machines. My daughter goes along in her off season from track and so that's a lot of fun."

My friend was quiet for a moment and then said, "I do that in my mind, and know I should go, but somehow never quite make it to the gym."

Intention is the road to nowhere. It's the pathway to not quite making it to the gym. Intention dead-ends your work.

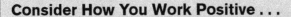

Consider How You Work Positive . . .

. . . and name one action you have intended to do,

 but just not done yet? Scan here to share online with the Work Positive Community

#culturecounts

Intention in Isolation

You discover in the next chapter how intention is a powerful catalyst when combined with attention and action. However, like all isolated catalysts, intention is ineffective in producing a reaction of any kind.

So, how do you recognize isolated intention? How do you know when your intention is just that—only an intention with no connection to attention or action?

Intention is a Burden

Isolated intention burdens you and slows you down instead of empowering you to Achieve positive results.

One summer, on Lake Isabella, located in the high desert an hour east of Bakersfield, California, some folks were new to boating and couldn't get their brand-new 22-footer going no matter how hard they tried. It was sluggish in every maneuver no matter how much they opened up the throttle.

After about an hour of trying to make it go, they putted to a nearby marina for a diagnostic. They had someone do a thorough topside check that found everything in perfect working condition. The engine ran fine. The outdrive went up and down. The prop was the correct size and pitch.

So, one of the marina guys jumped in the water to check underneath, and came up choking on water, he was laughing so hard. Under the boat, still strapped securely in place, was the trailer.

Intention is like that trailer. It has no propulsion system of its own. It carries your attention, pulled by the vehicle of action. Action is the engine. Isolated intention is a burden, slowing you down from Achieving the impossible so you can Work Positive.

Consider How You Work Positive . . .

What is your trailer or burden of an undone action that you are attached to? Scan here to share online with the Work Positive Community

#culturecounts

Intention Seeks Perfection Immediately

When you do act, intention seeks perfection immediately. You want to do something perfectly right now without giving the requisite time and attention to prepare for action. Work mistakes seem fatal. Your teammates know it because you refuse to tolerate anything that smells like a mistake. Your customers and clients know it because even when you make one, you fail to admit it. You blame everyone else before you take responsibility for it.

I can relate. I wanted to learn to play the guitar when I was a teenager. I saved some money, bought a guitar, and took lessons.

The guitar was beautiful and sounded amazing when my instructor played it . . . but my experience with it was a little different. I just couldn't make the music come out of the guitar that my teacher did. I practiced for hours, trying not to make mistakes, which meant that I'd get to the same place in a song and make the same mistake every time. My teacher said, "Everybody makes mistakes. That's the way we learn." All I learned was that my favorite group, the Eagles, never called and picked Joe Walsh instead.

Eventually I put the guitar down and never picked it up again.

Since then I've learned that my instructor was right. The only people who fail to make mistakes are either dead or quit trying like I did. Everybody makes mistakes. They are opportunities to learn.

I intended to learn to play the guitar, but my perfectionism got in the way. I divorced my intention to play the guitar from giving my attention to it and action with it.

Intention Fears Failure

Isolated intention is the road to nowhere. It burdens you and seeks perfection.

It also fears failure.

Fear of failure paralyzes so many of us. It's why an opportunity is analyzed until it's vanished. Every successful person's story includes several chapters of failed, previous attempts.

Failure is an experience, not a person.

On New Year's Day, 1929, Georgia Tech played UCLA in the Rose Bowl. In that game, Roy Riggles recovered a fumble for UCLA. Riggles became confused and ran sixty-five yards in the wrong direction. One of his teammates outran him and tackled him just before he scored for the other team. When UCLA tried to punt, Tech blocked the kick and scored a safety.

That strange play came in the first half, and everyone watching the game was asking the same question: What will Coach Price do with Roy Riggles in the second half? Price concluded his halftime pep talk with: "Men, the same team that played the first half starts the second."

"Coach," Riggles said, "I can't do it. I couldn't face that crowd in the stadium to save my life."

Coach Price said, "Roy, get up and go on back out there. The game is only half over."

Coach Price understood that failure is a play in the game rather than the game itself.

Keep playing.

Consider How You Work Positive . . .

What are you most afraid of failing at while you attempt to do it? Scan here to share online with the Work Positive Community

#culturecounts

Intention Gives Up and Quits

Your fear of failure drives your work excuses. You intend to take action and fear you will fail, forgetting that failure is an experience and the work game continues. Failure is actually not an option when you Perceive, Conceive, and Believe the positive at work. You choose to focus your thoughts on the positive at work, surround yourself with a team of positive people with whom you collaborate to do the work, and hold fast to the belief that you will create a positive work culture. And that's when you act. Yes, your actions zig and zag, are inefficient at times, and messy at others. Yet you Achieve the positive. Your positive outcome often happens in a way other than the one you originally thought.

This assurance means that the role of intention becomes one of continuing to work even when the path zigs and zags. Perseverance is the key. Isolated from attention and action, intention gives up.

Walter Johnson was a legendary baseball pitcher, a pitching phenomenon in his time, striking out batters at will.

A rookie faced Johnson for the first time. The rookie had two strikes called on him before he knew what happened. He just shook his head and walked away.

The umpire took off his mask and called after the rookie, "Son, where are you going? That was just strike two."

"You keep the third strike," the rookie said. "I've seen enough."

It happens. You see enough at work and you just want to walk away and just want to say to your boss and teammates, customers and clients, "You keep it."

Stay in the batter's box, even when you think you'll strike out. You only learn how to quit when you walk away. You learn something when you persevere—about yourself, about the situation, and what it takes to Achieve a positive work culture.

Intention Underestimates the Power of One

Intention is the road to nowhere when divorced from attention and action. Alone, it underestimates the power you have as one person who Perceives, Conceives, and Believes and therefore can Achieve the impossible at work.

Is it a challenge for you to Believe that as one person you can help transform the work culture from toxic to positive?

Small hinges swing big doors.

One person can make a huge difference.

I traveled to do onsite coaching with an executive. Something unusual happened while I was there. A city employee accidentally spilled about a cup of hydraulic oil into the city's water supply. An emergency bulletin was broadcast, letting us all know that while we could bathe, we couldn't drink the water even if we boiled it.

I didn't think much about it until I went to lunch and discovered that I could only order bottled water. That evening I found that homemade bread was unavailable. The next morning, we couldn't get coffee. Bottles and jugs of water flew off store shelves.

One person's adventure in learning how to keep hydraulic oil out of the city's water supply paralyzed a major metropolitan area for most of a day, transforming the way we ate, drank, and even bathed. Intention—"I didn't mean to spill the oil"—had no effect on the outcome of this one person's action. His attention and action were misguided from his intention. Intention by itself underestimates the power of one person to transform work culture.

Consider How You Work Positive . . .

What have you Perceived, Conceived, and Believed that you could Achieve, but refused to pursue because you are "just one person?" Scan here to share online with the Work Positive Community
#culturecounts

Intention Rushes to Results

What you meant to do and failed to do burdens you. It seeks perfection immediately, short-circuiting your learning the unfamiliar. It fears failure, which shuts your action down, causing you to give up. It underestimates the power that you as one person have to transform the work culture.

Intention without attention and action rushes to results..

I enjoy growing roses. I noticed one day that almost all the blooms had faded and that even though there were plenty of buds, the bushes lacked any open flowers.

I thought, "I wish these rose buds would hurry up and open, or, at least part of them. I wish there was something I could to do to speed them up."

Then it occurred to me that there is no way to unfold a rose bud more quickly without destroying it. Sure, I can water it regularly and feed it often, but I simply destroy a rose bud when I attempt to open it with my hands. The rose bush is damaged when rushed.

Intention when separated from attention and action rushes you through your work experiences—through tough times, easy times and all the times in between. Top talent turns down your offer. Teams lose members. Your productivity lessens. Your profits shrink.

You must slow down to speed up.

Dynamic work growth happens as you Perceive, Conceive, and Believe. Your work's best traits emerge. Your core values, priorities, and unique contribution shine clearly into your business relationships. It is as you slow down, that the challenges of each moment present themselves as opportunities destined for your Work Positive culture success. You do more than survive. You thrive.

You slow down to speed up. Your work habits strengthen despite the adversity.

The Great Barrier Reef stretches some 1,800 miles from New Guinea to Australia. The lagoon side of the reef looks pale and lifeless, while the ocean side is vibrant and colorful. The reason for this phenomenon is that the coral on the lagoon side is in still water with no challenge for its survival. It dies early. The coral on the ocean side is constantly tested by wind, waves, and storms—surges of power. It fights for survival every day of its life. It changes and adapts as it is challenged and tested. It grows healthier and stronger every day.

You are like that coral as you learn to Work Positive. Work comes alive and grows when challenged and tested by adverse storms. The untested aspects of your work intend to grow, and yet unchallenged, atrophy. The challenged side confronts adversity daily and grows. That which could be seen as negative becomes the opportunity for growing your Work Positive culture in what you may think of as the worst of times.

Here is the key to understanding the true power of intention: Your intention to Work Positive is the road to nowhere when left alone, unchallenged. Intention is a powerful catalyst when partnered with attention and action. Just like the ocean stimulates the coral, intention builds a positive vitality of successful culture.

Consider How You Work Positive . . .

. . . and name one challenge you are experiencing right now in your work that, like the ocean, can be a source of stimulation and vitality for you. Scan here to share online with the Work Positive Community
#culturecounts

Grab & Go

Intention is the Road to Nowhere and helps you develop your Work Positive work culture:

1. Let your "Yes" mean "Yes" and your "No" mean "No."
2. A trailer of burden definitely slows your work down.
3. Perfection is the enemy of playing the guitar. . .or anything else you want to do.
4. Stay in the batter's box and swing at all the opportunities thrown in your team's strike zone.
5. You have the power as one person to transform work culture.
6. Impatiently rushing to results destroys the rose bud in your work that blossoms in due time.
7. Your work grows best when tested and challenged.

chapter 16

Take the Prescription for Achievement

"Action is the foundational key to all success."
—Pablo Picasso

One summer, I decided that the shrubs at one end of our home had grown too tall. So, I got out the chainsaw and cut them back. It took a while because they were tall and thick, but eventually I got down to the main trunk. All I left was a stump.

Our daughters asked, "Daddy, why did you kill the bushes?"

"I didn't kill them. I cut them back," I said.

"No, Daddy, you killed them."

"Watch them," I said. "Soon you'll see tiny green shoots coming out of them. And by this time next year, they'll be covered with greenery."

"No, they won't, Daddy. You killed them."

Well, the next spring arrived, and slowly but surely, green shoots emerged from those "dead" stumps. Just a few at first, then more, and soon they were full again.

The shrubs survived the pruning and thrived.

Your efforts to Achieve the positive at work by isolated intention make you appear like those shrubs I cut back. Your work looks dead. You look around and wonder why the economic conditions mowed you down, what you did to deserve such a slow sales period. You search for someone, anyone to blame— your teammates and customers, your clients and vendors, the President and Congress. You avoid taking personal responsibility for your lack of attention and action because your bent to ego rarely tolerates such imperfection. You compare your work to others and compete with them in an effort to fortify your deficit of positive results. "At least my work is better off than theirs," you tell yourself. You retreat into the familiar and take solace in your memories that once upon a time you succeeded.

Intention is a catalyst. It requires mixing with attention and action for you to Achieve the impossible at work as you Perceive, Conceive, and Believe it.

Consider How You Work Positive . . .

When was a time that you regarded your work the way my daughters did the shrubs? Recall your recovery from that mile marker experience. How did it happen? What was it like? Scan here to share online with the Work Positive Community

#culturecounts

The Importance of Action

Attention plus intention is an excellent beginning to Achieve the positive at work, to invigorate the thoughts you Perceive as positive, Conceive with other positive people, and Believe will happen as you imagine the very best for your work. It's how you start to attract top talent and reduce team turnover so you create a positive work culture that increases productivity and profits.

There is still one missing ingredient in your prescription for achieving your Work Positive culture. That missing element is action.

Action delivers achievement.

Hear the vitality of action in these universal truths:

"Ask and you'll receive."

"Knock and it'll open."

"Seek and you'll find it."

Each begins with an active verb.

You have to do something to get positive results.

What if these statements read instead:

"Sit there with your mouth closed, expect people to read your mind, and you'll receive."

"Just stand there, staring at the door, and it'll open for you."

"Relax in your favorite recliner and see what shows up on your front porch."

Sure, you may give some attention to the situation, and you intend to do something about it. Yet you fail to create a Work Positive culture until you act.

The Prescription to Achieve Work Positive Results

Here's how you Work Positive once you Perceive, Conceive, and Believe:

Attention + Intention + ACTION = Achieve a Work Positive culture

What you considered impossible happens as you work this prescription.

Attention is the attraction factor for your mental energy as you Perceive. You focus and filter your thoughts and concentrate on an identified work priority like a goal. Your attention attracts others like your teammates and customers with whom you Conceive, your social investment in the goal. You Believe that it can happen and share the belief that this reality can be redefined, and the goal realized.

Intention is the catalyst that carries your attention like a trailer. Hitched to a vehicle, the trailer carries a boat. Then you back into the lake, unhook the boat from the trailer, and crank up the motor of action.

The Impossible Becomes Possible When You Act

I drove to the Washington, DC, area to do a speaking engagement. I left early, knowing that traffic in Northern Virginia slows me down. I had no idea how slow that would be until I arrived on a major highway that quickly became a parking lot. Road construction all around us pushed traffic from many lanes to a couple.

I looked into my rearview mirror as I sat in traffic. I saw a huge motor grader heading toward me. It was one of those vehicles that carry tons of dirt from one place to another. It kept coming toward me without turning. It filled my rearview mirror. Soon all I could see was the front of this huge dirt mover.

I imagined what would be said at my funeral—"He was a good man who didn't have sense enough to get out of the way of a motor grader."

At what seemed like the last possible moment, that gigantic earth mover turned off to the right, onto the lane under construction, and continued another couple of hundred yards and stopped. I breathed a prayer of thanks, and then looked closer. A door opened on the tiny cab and out popped a guy who was about five foot, two inches tall, and probably weighed 140 pounds.

I thought, "If I asked a group of people if a 5' 2", 140-pound man could move ten tons of dirt singlehandedly, most of them would respond, 'No way.'"

And yet he did the impossible.

He did the Work Positive prescription:

Attention + Intention + ACTION = Achieve Work Positive culture.

If he did it, so can you.

Consider How You Work Positive . . .

. . . and name one aspect of your current work reality that you want redefined, no matter how impossible it appears to you right now. What dream is fulfilled for you when that reality is redefined? Take a moment and write it down. Scan here to share online with the Work Positive Community

#culturecounts

How Do You Act Best?

So, how do you do it? How do you best act on your work priorities?

Here are two keys:

1. Constant collaboration, and;

2. Work Positive regardless.

Constant Collaboration

Constant collaboration is the result of your action.

You march off your mental map into uncharted territory when you avoid only familiar thoughts. You cease using Eeyore Vampires as a reference point and Conceive with others when you compare and compete rarely. You begin to imagine the best possible outcomes when you Believe and resist your bent to ego. You discover that some of your actions produce dramatic results as you act to create a Work Positive culture.

Constant collaboration evaluates your actions. It is an opportunity for course correction. Think of constant collaboration as your work's GPS.

I usually leave my garage by typing my destination in Google Maps and touching "Start." The device decides where I am, where I want to go, and the best route for getting there. It directs me where and when to turn. I program it to avoid toll roads, to take interstates or scenic routes, and find my favorite restaurants along the way.

It recalculates and advises me accordingly when I take an unrecommended turn. She says something like "Please make a U-turn when legal" or gives me the best street to turn on to get back on route. So far, she has yet to call me an idiot or a fool, or ask me "What were you thinking?" or "Are you asleep or stupid?" She just recalculates and redirects.

Your Inner Critic is not that generous. Your Inner Critic wants you to call yourself an idiot or a fool when you make a mistake.

There may be Eeyore Vampires on your team who ask, "What were you thinking? Oh, wait, you weren't," or your boss who says, "Are you asleep or stupid?" when your efforts fall short at work.

Avoid placing a value judgment on yourself by listening to your Inner Critic. Turn a deaf ear to the Eeyore Vampires and yes, sometimes the boss. Pay close attention to the constant collaboration around those most-effective actions and pursue them. Do those actions more often in your day-to-day work. Facilitate the results as just that—results—and feed them back into how you Perceive, Conceive, and Believe for future actions. "Recalculate" and do what works best to get you back on the preferred path of a Work Positive culture.

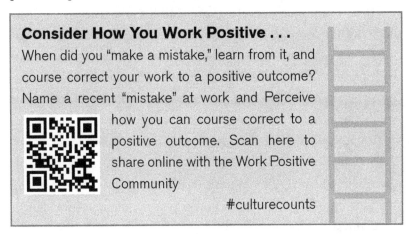

Consider How You Work Positive . . .
When did you "make a mistake," learn from it, and course correct your work to a positive outcome? Name a recent "mistake" at work and Perceive how you can course correct to a positive outcome. Scan here to share online with the Work Positive Community

#culturecounts

Work Positive Regardless

The second important action factor, Work Positive regardless, comes into play next. At times you allow negativity to creep into your thoughts instead of "recalculate." You invite Eeyore Vampires into the circle of people with whom you Conceive. You let the "can't do its" leap into what you Believe. You compare and compete and practice "negative conceiving." You, me, and all of us want to quit at these times.

It is at this very intersection that you Work Positive regardless. You move forward anyway. You persevere and act to Achieve a Work Positive culture.

The longer I coach and study the traits of those who create a Work Positive culture, the more convinced I am that the choice to persevere and act is essential.

Some famous examples include Abraham Lincoln who went bankrupt as a business owner and lost more political elections than he won on his way to the White House and salvaging our war-torn nation. Jerry Seinfeld forgot all his jokes the first time he did stand-up comedy, got fired from a TV show because he could not act, and had his show cancelled on the way to becoming one of the highest paid comedians in the world. Michael Jordan was cut from the basketball team at Laney High School in Wilmington, North Carolina, in his freshman year along the way to becoming what many consider the best basketball player in modern history. Thomas Edison survived a laboratory fire that destroyed all his notes with some 1,999 ways not to make a light bulb in creating the light bulb. John Grisham sold copies of his first book out of the trunk of his car in Charlottesville, Virginia, and other places he could drive between court cases before achieving the title of "best-selling author." Tom Landry, Chuck Noll, and Bill Walsh accounted for nine of the fifteen Super Bowl victories from 1974 to 1989. They also had the worst records of first-season head coaches in NFL history. Test pilot Chuck Yeager said, "I have learned to back up, but I never give up."

Consider How You Work Positive . . .

Who is someone you know who was tempted to give up, but did not, and achieved positive results?

 Tell that person's story right now. Scan here to share online with the Work Positive Community

#culturecounts

You can back up but not give up like Chuck Yeager and all these other persons who Achieved positive results. You Perceive, Conceive, and Believe to create a Work Positive culture, and then act regardless to Achieve it. You transform the impossible into the possible through constant collaboration and Working Positive regardless. That's how you attract top talent and reduce team turnover so you create a positive work culture that increases productivity and profits.

Achieve Work Positive Results

The Work Positive culture you Achieve is simple to do and yet equally profound.

I visited a friend in the hospital who had cancer. I had just walked in when the nurse appeared in the doorway, and said to my friend, "I'm sorry, we don't have any."

My friend looked at me and said, "I'll bet you're wondering what I requested. Toothpicks. I asked if they had any toothpicks. I just love my toothpicks after I eat."

I thought to myself walking down the hall after our visit, "There she is, dying from cancer, and all she wants is a toothpick." As I rode down the elevator, the thought hit me, "Go get her a box of toothpicks. It's such a little thing."

So, I went to the grocery store, bought a box of toothpicks, and went back to the hospital, where she was eating her supper, and said, "I have just what you'll want after your meal" and handed her the toothpicks. I will always remember her look of surprise and laughter.

Small hinges swing big doors.

Simple acts become profound as you create a Work Positive culture.

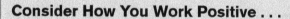

Consider How You Work Positive . . .

What is something simple you can do for a co-worker that will be profound? Scan here to share online with the Work Positive Community

#culturecounts

Resources converge in mysterious ways as you persevere and act.

A client's insurance agency is just a few blocks from a high school. One day, a student walked in and asked to speak with the owner. My client met her, and she said, "I'm in the Distributive Education program at my school down the street and I need a job. It has to be a job I can walk to since I'm only 15 and can't drive. You don't have to pay me. I need to work six hours a week."

He was so impressed that one so young walked right in and asked for a job that he gave it to her on the spot. "Nobody works for me for free," he told her. He paid her for the six hours each week.

Her hours increased as did her salary.

She worked her way through high school and then college. She graduated with a degree in fashion design. Once college was only an impossible dream. She did a design internship in Europe, finished college, and now works in California for a fashion designer.

All because she paid attention to what businesses were nearby, intended to stop by, and acted by stepping through the door of my client's business and asked for a job.

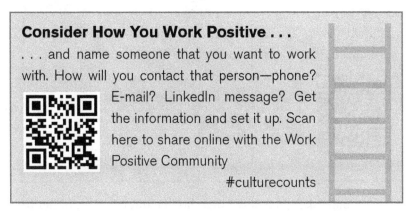

Consider How You Work Positive . . .

. . . and name someone that you want to work with. How will you contact that person—phone? E-mail? LinkedIn message? Get the information and set it up. Scan here to share online with the Work Positive Community

#culturecounts

Resources converge in mysterious ways as you persevere and act.

The six-year-old daughter of a client discovered that I live with horses on our farm and got really excited. She asked our horses' names and wanted to know what they looked like. I said, "Do you like horses?"

"Yes, I do," she said. "I went to horse camp last summer."

"You did?" I said. "Was it fun?"

"You betcha," she said. "The teacher told me that it's hard to ride ponies. They're hard to handle. But they weren't hard for me. I thought they were easy."

"Why were they easy for you?" I said.

She said, "I didn't believe the teacher. I just got on and rode."

My six-year-old friend, born to Believe, chose to imagine the best which meant persevering and acting like riding a pony is easy to ride despite what the Eeyore Vampire instructor said. She Achieved the impossible.

Resources converge in mysterious ways as you persevere and act.

Consider How You Work Positive . . .

What Eeyore Vampire have you allowed to block you imagining the best? Choose right now to disbelieve this Eeyore Vampire. What will you do to just get on and ride your opportunity? Scan here to share online with the Work Positive Community

#culturecounts

Our older daughter was a preschooler and had a lot of her toys scattered on the floor. I asked her to please pick them up.

"I don't want to, Daddy," she said. "I'm too tired."

I looked at her with my "You don't really expect me to believe that" look. She looked back with her "Please fall for that line" look.

So, I said, "Well, you will pick up your toys, but what if we play a game first?"

"OK," she said.

"What about 'Ride the horsey?'" I asked. That was her favorite game with me at the time. It's the one where you put the child on your leg and "Ride the horsey down to town, better watch out 'cause you might fall down" and then lower the child to floor.

She climbed up in my lap and rode the horsey a couple of times. Then I said, "Now clean up your toys and we'll ride the horsey one more time."

She put her toys away in about 90 seconds. She wasn't too tired to ride the horsey again, either.

Working positive regardless is challenging at times. Some days you face something at work you want to avoid or at least procrastinate. In those moments, it is just fine to play, and then Work Positive. You know what they say about "all work and no play." The road to creating a positive work culture can be fun, also!

Consider How You Work Positive . . .

Who is someone else you know who was tempted to give up, refused, and achieved positive results?

 Tell yourself that person's story right now. Scan here to share online with the Work Positive Community #culturecounts

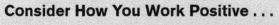

As you act on your work intentions which have your attention, the positive results you Perceived, Conceived, and Believed could happen actually do. Your reality redefines and realigns to fulfill your dreams. Top talent joins your teams. Team members stay. Productivity and profits increase. Your Work Positive culture emerges even in a negative world.

And that's when you wonder, "What do I do next?"

Let's discover the fifth and final core practice of your Work Positive culture.

Grab & Go

Take the Prescription for Achievement.

1. Attention + Intention + ACTION = Achieve Work Positive culture
2. Ask to receive. Knock to open. Seek to find.
3. A 140-pound man can move ten tons of dirt.
4. Listen to and follow your Work Positive GPS. Then recalculate your route to increased productivity and profits.
5. Work Positive regardless like Abraham Lincoln, Jerry Seinfeld, Michael Jordan, Thomas Edison, John Grisham, Tom Landry, Chuck Noll, Bill Walsh, and Chuck Yeager.
6. Buy toothpicks for a friend. Ask for a job and go to college. Just get on the horse and ride into your Work Positive culture.
7. Ride the horsey down to town first. Then pick up your toys. Play!

Core Practice 5:

RECEIVE the POSITIVE at Work

chapter 17

You Can Receive the Positive at Work

"The thing that lies at the foundation of positive change, the way I see it, is service to a fellow human being."
—Lech Walesa

When my wife was pregnant with our first child, she really wanted a certain kind of baby crib—the Jenny Lind crib.

I didn't have enough money to buy it, but I wanted to purchase it because it meant that much to my wife. I was discovering even then how to Work Positive.

First, I remembered my shotgun. I had not been hunting for years with that gun, but it was still special to me. Santa Claus brought it to me when I was thirteen years old. It was my "dream gun"—a Remington 870 Wingmaster pump action 12 gauge with a twenty-eight-inch modified choke barrel. I drooled all over "her page" in the Sears Wishbook catalog that year. I stood for hours staring at her in the local gun shop. Not that I was attached to my gun or anything like that . . .

I decided to sell the gun and buy the baby crib. I stopped by to visit my friend, James, on my way to the gun shop to sell it. He said he wanted it. So, I sold the shotgun to him and bought the crib, presenting it to my wife as a surprise baby gift.

About fourteen years later my wife threw me a huge birthday party for my fortieth. She had about 250 of my closest friends over for a meal and party.

She escorted me into our home after everyone left and said, "There's one more thing. Close your eyes and hold out your hands and I will give you a big surprise."

I did, and then she said, "OK, open your eyes! Here's your birthday present" and handed me MY Remington Wingmaster twelve-gauge shotgun that I had sold to buy the Jenny Lind baby crib.

"Where did you get it?" I said.

"From James," she said. "I called him and told him that you were turning forty and asked him if I could buy your gun back. And Joey," she said. "He wouldn't let me pay him. He gave it to me as your present."

When you Perceive, Conceive, Believe, and Achieve a Work Positive culture and share it with others, you Receive back more of the same.

The first core practice is you Perceive your Work Positive culture and focus on the positive at work, avoid only familiar thoughts, and filter your thoughts.

The second core practice is you Conceive the positive at work and attract your dream team, customers and clients, and others based on your core values, work priorities, and unique contribution. Together you cooperate, compare and compete rarely, and collaborate.

The third core practice is you Believe the positive at work and redefine your work reality and claim your birthright to Believe, avoid your bent to ego, and imagine your work culture at its best.

The fourth core practice is you Achieve the positive at work and pay attention to important thoughts and people, align your intention to Believe, and act to achieve a Work Positive culture.

The fifth core practice, Receive, is about the unique rewards and delightful experiences you have as you say, "Thank you," squeeze yourself dry, and serve others.

chapter 18

Say "Thank You"

"It's nice to help remember somebody who really made a very positive difference in the world."
—Mary Hart

One day, a small card showed up in the mail and found its way to my desk. I opened it and it read:

Dear Dr. Joey,
You don't know me and we'll probably never meet personally. I was in the audience at a speaking engagement you did. I was a mess that day. My business was dying. I was ready to quit.
You changed my life. After listening to you, I found the way to Work Positive and the motivation to do it.
I just wanted to say thank you for saving my business and my life.

What I learned from a person I don't even remember meeting was this: two little words—"thank you"—are among the most powerful on the planet. They grow exponentially more powerful when written personally, by someone's hand holding an ink pen.

181

Yes, your Work Positive culture transformation requires a ton of energy and effort by you to Perceive, Conceive, Believe, and Achieve positive outcomes. At the end of the day, you simply find a way to say, "thank you" to your tour guides and fellow tourists who invested in you along the work journey because you realize that you Received the positive, too.

Consider How You Work Positive . . .

Recall the last handwritten thank-you note you received. What was it for? Who was it from? Now remember the last handwritten thank-you note you mailed. Having a little difficulty remembering? Find a note card or a piece of paper and write a thank-you note to someone from whom you Received something positive. Scan here to share online with the Work Positive Community

#culturecounts

Givers Gain®

Ivan Misner, the founder of BNI (Business Network International), created this franchised referral network of business people on the philosophy of Givers Gain®. That is, work is wired so that when you give to others—in this case, when you refer business to other members in your chapter—you literally gain more business because you give.

Think about your own work for a moment. Have you ever said, "I went to help him out, and he helped me more"? Or, "I told Suzie about John and how he's a great guy to buy a car from, and six people showed up in my store the other day saying John sent them"?

That's how it works. Givers Gain®.

You discovered something as you Work Positive from these core practices and Perceive, Conceive, Believe, and Achieve positive results. You also Receive positive results.

So, what do you do with these positive outcomes?

Any broken-arm back-patting going on? Sure, you rerouted neural pathways, kicked the Eeyore Vampires to the curb, imagined the best, and acted on your attention and intention. You are starting to transform to a Work Positive culture.

And yet everything you did was guided.

You learned how your mind works best and acted accordingly.

Yet did you create your brain?

You discovered how to work for collaboration in your team relationships. Yet did you seek out all the positive people on your team? Many found you.

You realized that you were born to believe and could actually imagine work at its best. And yet did you give birth to yourself?

You recognized that as you paid more attention to positive thoughts and people, coupled it to your intentions, and acted, a Work Positive culture emerged, showing up on the faces of your satisfied customers and clients, in handwritten thank you notes, and in the looks of gratitude teammates give you.

Yes, you are an integral player in the new Work Positive culture. Yet did you act alone? Positive results showed up that are unexplainable, right?

Resources converge as you act.

You Work Positive from these first four core practices to the best of your ability, and yet as your Work Positive culture appears, you Receive.

Consider How You Work Positive . . .

What is one positive result you received while reading this book? Scan here to share online with the Work Positive Community

#culturecounts

Think about it this way. When you say, "What goes around, comes around" or "You reap what you sow," what do you mean?

Givers Gain®, right?

You Receive your Work Positive culture.

So, what else can you say except "Thank you!" as you Receive?

How Do You Say "Thank You" to Your Customers?

Your attitude towards work transforms to gratitude once you realize that you Receive. You want to say, "Thank you!" to someone. What about starting with your customers?

One of my favorite books is Tim Sanders' *Love Is the Killer App: How to Win Business and Influence Friends*. He tells the story of his friend Mike, who was president of Pizza Hut. Mike called his MVCs—Most Valuable Customers—every Friday during his lunch hour to say, "thank you for your business."

Mike called a customer in a poor neighborhood in south Dallas who ordered more than a dozen large pizzas a month for a year. "From the bottom of my heart," he told her, "I want to thank you for your business." Then he asked the mother, "Tell me why you order our pizza. What's your story?"

The mother told Mike her story of being a divorced mother of five children, aged three to eleven, and of how she worked three jobs to support them. She didn't want her kids to see their mom accepting public assistance, so she worked virtually nonstop. She let the eldest order pizza as a kind of reward because "my kids really love your pizza."

Mike was so moved by her story that he said, "Ma'am, I want to thank you for something entirely different than being a good customer. I want to thank you for being a good mother."

Who will this mother buy pizza from for the rest of her life? How many of her friends will she tell this story of the day the president of Pizza Hut thanked her for being a good mother? How many pizzas will they buy?

Will Mike tell that story with a misty eye to his team with whom he Conceives a Work Positive culture to remind them of how much they can Believe in Pizza Hut as they Achieve the positive at work? Mike called to give and gained.

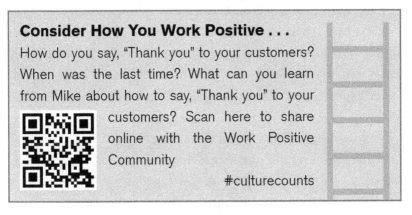

Consider How You Work Positive . . .
How do you say, "Thank you" to your customers? When was the last time? What can you learn from Mike about how to say, "Thank you" to your customers? Scan here to share online with the Work Positive Community

#culturecounts

Saying "thank you" to your customers deepens your relationships and everyone Receives.

How Do You Say "Thank You" to Your Teammates?

A friend was the general manager of a rapidly growing manufacturing company. One day over lunch, we discussed how to say, "thank you" to co-workers rather than assume we exchange money for their time.

We talked about time off for family experiences like ball games and a grandbaby's birth. We mentioned flowers on Valentine's Day and other gifts on holidays.

Then we turned to the gift of presence that responds in more than the anticipated life events. He told the story of how an employee was on the brink of financial disaster due to unforeseen life events. She had come to the operations manager about the situation and explained she may not be at her best productivity because of the stress. The ops manager shared the predicament with my GM friend who asked, "How much does she need?"

The OM said something about her inability to pay it back, but my friend simply said again, "How much does she need?"

The OM stated the amount, and my friend said, "Give it to her and tell her to pay it back as she can."

She paid it back as she could, a little at a time, and is now one of the most productive employees in the company. She constantly brags on her employer and how much management cares for its employees. She helps the company attract top talent which increases productivity and profits even more.

My friend gave and gained even more.

Sure, not every company can lend money to its employees. Most of the time a listening ear or big shoulder to lean on is enough and costs little. Investing your ears and shoulders in your teammates is one way of saying "thank you."

Consider How You Work Positive . . .

How do you say, "thank you" to your teammates? What other ways can you deepen your relationship with your co-workers so that more of you say, "Thank you!"? Scan here to share online with the Work Positive Community

#culturecounts

This Book is My Thanks to You

My motive in writing this book has nothing to do with bestseller lists, or speaking tours or monetary rewards, or the stuff those rewards make possible. Maybe it should and sure, they are nice, and yet . . .

. . . my motive is to coach you to create a Work Positive culture so you attract top talent and reduce team turnover and increase productivity and profits.

We must all work together to transform the negative world into a Work Positive Nation filled with dream-achievers. This transformation is less about "me" and more about "we."

Thank you for investing your mental, social, emotional, physical, and ethical energies in positive ways at work because of what you read.

Thank you for imagining how much better our work cultures become as more and more of us say, "Thank you!"

Say, "Thank you!" as you Receive and Work Positive.

Consider How You Work Positive . . .

Who is one person you know that could use a copy of this book and help you create a more positive work culture where "Thank you" is heard often? Scan here to share online with the Work Positive Community

#culturecounts

Grab & Go

Remember these as you "Say Thank You."

1. Write a personal, handwritten "thank you" to someone at least once a week. Be specific with your gratitude.
2. "Givers Gain®." (Dr. Ivan Misner, BNI)
3. "What goes around, comes around."
4. "You reap what you sow."
5. You Receive as you Work Positive.
6. This book is about you creating a Work Positive culture.
7. Simply say, "Thank you," to everyone associated with your work as often as possible.

chapter 19

Squeeze Yourself Dry

"You cannot live a perfect day without doing something for
someone who will never be able to repay you."
—John Wooden

Ｉf you put a sponge under running water, within a few minutes it
is saturated. It can hold no more water.

But what if you left the sponge under the running water for
five more minutes? Would it hold any more?

Perhaps if you left the sponge under the running water for a
whole day it would hold more.

How about if you left it under the running water for a whole
week? Would it hold any more?

What would you have to do for the sponge to hold more water?

Squeeze it out. Only when you squeeze the sponge will it hold
more water.

You are like a sponge as you create a Work Positive culture.
You soak up more when you squeeze your work and give away the
positive results you receive. You create room within your work for
increased productivity and profits.

Consider How You Work Positive . . .

. . . and recall the last time you squeezed yourself and shared your positive results. Maybe you gave some surplus product to a benevolence group. Perhaps you chaired an American Cancer Society fundraiser. Or, you gave frequent flyer miles to a young couple to use on their honeymoon. Or, some other squeezing occasion . . . what did you do? Scan here to share online with the Work Positive Community

#culturecounts

How Can Someone Hand You Something . . .

. . . if your hands are full?

What if you want something a teammate hands you more than what you are holding? What will you do?

You empty your hands to receive it.

Your hands are full if you hang on to your most recent positive achievement so long that you begin to claim solo credit for it. You receive only the accolades and applause that accompany the experience. You deny yourself and your work associates the next great positive experience.

There is a penalty in college football for "bringing too much attention to oneself" after scoring. This rule intends to develop good sportsmanship among these young men in stark contrast to NFL players. They begin their egotistical antics before they score and continue after the play to gain more celebrity status.

As in football, so it is as you create a Work Positive culture.

You make habits of the first four core practices of Perceive, Conceive, Believe, and Achieve to the best of your ability. You squeeze yourself dry so more culture transformation happens for you, your team, and the company. You share the credit and other benefits with the team so top talent joins, team members stay and productivity and profits increase. Work Positive is a team sport.

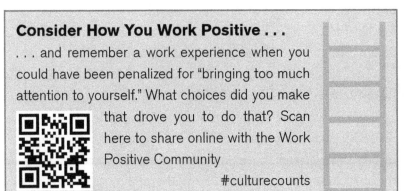

Consider How You Work Positive . . .

. . . and remember a work experience when you could have been penalized for "bringing too much attention to yourself." What choices did you make that drove you to do that? Scan here to share online with the Work Positive Community

#culturecounts

Who Is Squeezing Whom?

A client requested a meeting with his banker one day and the conversation went something like this:

As you know, I have always paid on time when you loaned me money. I've always been very conscientious about making my payments. However, currently I find myself in a bit of a jam. The people who owe me money are not paying at all instead of just a little late. I'm here today to request that you restructure my debt, extending the term, and giving me a grace period of 30 extra days to come up with a payment.

The banker agreed to the terms, had the contract drawn up, and both lender and borrower were satisfied.

The relieved client left the bank and saw someone who owed him money walking on the other side of the street.

"Hey!" he yelled loudly enough for everyone on Main Street to hear. "Come here. You owe me money!"

He ran across the street, grabbed the guy's arm and said, "Where's my money? You think you can just take my money and not pay it back? That's a crime, my friend."

He forced the man into a nearby magistrate's office, filed a complaint, and had the man thrown into jail.

The banker heard some commotion on Main Street from his third-floor corner office and lifted the window to see what was happening. He watched in horror as the client that he just forgave his previous terms of payment accosted another man, drug him into the magistrate's office, and emerged alone. The banker knew the magistrate, so he called to inquire about the incident and discovered that the client had the man imprisoned.

The banker then said to the magistrate, "Well, I have a complaint of my own to file." He rescinded the extension of terms for the client, and had the magistrate swear out a warrant for his arrest. Before the day was over, the client was in the jail cell next to the man he had imprisoned.

What goes around, comes around.

You reap what you sow.

Consider How You Work Positive . . .

. . . and recall a work experience when you failed to pass on the positive results you received. What was the outcome for you? For others? Scan here to share online with the Work Positive Community #culturecounts

Remember There is Enough

Like this client, you are tempted to keep positive results to yourself in fear that your work runs dry. You choose the scarcity mentality of "There's not enough to go around!" The scarcity mindset believes, "I got mine and so you get yours" because there are a limited number of profitable slices of work pie.

Of course, this mental model is the antithesis of the Work Positive culture. There is an abundance of resources that converge as you Believe and imagine the best your work can be. The pie has infinite slices as you Work Positive. You avoid running on empty.

I took my lawn mower to the shop for repairs, picked it up and brought it home, cranked it up and started mowing. The engine started choking and coughing after a couple of passes and finally just quit, and refused to restart.

You can imagine what I was thinking: "This mower just came back from the shop and now it doesn't work. Where's my phone?"

I called the repair shop, explained the mower's symptoms, and in as polite a voice as I could manage asked, "Now what's wrong with it?"

The kind, patient man with whom I was talking said, "Check the gas cap. There's a small screw valve on the top that we tighten down to keep the gas from spilling out when we turn the mower over. The gas doesn't get any air if we fail to open it. It's like it's running on empty."

Ever seem like your work is running on empty?

Check the valve of your focus. Odds are it's shifted from "Givers Gain®" to "Finders keepers, losers weepers." Instead, open the valve at work and let some positive air flow through you. Squeeze yourself dry.

Work Positive culture teams and companies are wired to support abundance as they Perceive, Conceive, Believe, and

Achieve positive results. It's when results are hoarded that the work culture grows negative.

Think about it like this: I lend you a million dollars. You agree to start making interest-free payments of $10,000 by the middle of each month after one year.

On the first of each month, I send you a check for $10,000 for you to make your monthly payment.

That's right. I make your monthly payment for you on the money I loaned you.

That's crazy, right?

The greatest challenge you have in squeezing yourself dry is to trust that as you squeeze, you will receive more.

Get over yourself. Trust the abundance around you. There is an infinite source of resources waiting to be yours as you create a Work Positive culture.

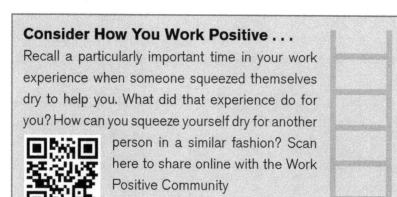

Consider How You Work Positive . . .

Recall a particularly important time in your work experience when someone squeezed themselves dry to help you. What did that experience do for you? How can you squeeze yourself dry for another person in a similar fashion? Scan here to share online with the Work Positive Community

#culturecounts

Anticipate the Unexpected

One thing to anticipate as you squeeze your work dry is you get unexpected reactions. Some of them are cut from the cloth of "Compare and Compete."

Clemson University's former football coach, Frank Howard, told the story of driving in Greenville, South Carolina, one day. He saw a bumper sticker on the car in front of him that read, "Honk if you love Jesus."

Howard said, "I love Jesus, so I honked."

When he did, the woman in the car with the bumper sticker on it, got out, shook her fist, and said, "You fool, you want me to smack you? Can't you see the light hasn't changed?"

Sometimes you get an unexpected reaction when you squeeze yourself dry. Sometimes what you do is misinterpreted by someone else. The other person doesn't "get" what you mean as you try to pass on what you Receive.

So, what do you do?

Explain when they will listen.

Ask for forgiveness when necessary.

Keep squeezing and honking.

Squeeze yourself dry and in gratitude share your Work Positive culture with others. Trust that there is plenty to go around. Discover that the more you give away, the more you Receive. You find more and more money, time, and opportunities at the end of every week, month, and year.

That's when you transform to the final Work Positive culture step of serving others.

Grab & Go

Remember to "Squeeze Yourself Dry" and:

1. Squeeze a sponge so it holds more water. Squeeze your work so it holds more Work Positive results.
2. Empty your hands to Receive.
3. Share the glory when you score.
4. When you are running on empty, your work focus shifted from "Givers Gain®" to "Finders keepers, losers weepers."
5. You Receive all you need at work and more as you Perceive, Conceive, Believe, and Achieve.
6. There are more slices in the pie chart of your work than you can eat in a lifetime.
7. Anticipate the unexpected. Honk anyway.

chapter 20

Serve Others

"We make a living by what we get,
but we make a life by what we give."
—Winston Churchill

O ne spring I hung a bird feeder in an oak tree just outside my office window. I really like watching cardinals and there are lots of them in our part of the world.

I looked them up on the internet and discovered they prefer sunflower seeds and put lots of them in the feeder. I attracted about a dozen different families of cardinals to my feeder.

The key is offering them what they prefer. I wanted them to come and visit me, so I gave them what they wanted.

You Receive as you give. It's a universal principle woven into the fabric of your Work Positive culture. Think of it as the Law of Reciprocity.

Givers Gain®.

What goes around comes around.

You reap what you sow.

Have an Attitude of Gratitude

Another key is to give and Receive motivated by thanksgiving. Your work now prospers as you create a Work Positive culture. You Work Positive to attract top talent and reduce team turnover. So, you serve these teams from an attitude of gratitude. You give thanks for what you Receive at work by offering customers what they prefer.

The ways in which you serve others are uniquely yours. Your unique contribution to the culture emanates from your passion, gifts, and personality also serves to meet the needs of teams. It's at the corner of your contribution and the world's needs that your Work Positive work culture does business.

I talked with a man who runs a dry-cleaning business. I asked him, "What do you find most fulfilling about what you do?"

He told me the story about how a family's home burned. One of the only things salvaged was the little girl's teddy bear and it was in pretty rough shape with soot and stains all over him. He was soaked from the fire hoses and did not smell very good. The little girl absolutely loved this teddy bear and it was all she had left after the fire.

This business owner took on the mission of cleaning up the teddy bear. He worked on the little bear's soot stains until they were gone. He cleaned up and sanitized the bear so that he smelled good. The dry cleaner said, "That was one happy little girl when I was through."

He went on to say, "And that's why I love to do what I do. I get to make a difference."

This man serves others, meets needs, by making his unique contribution as he Works Positive. His service drives his work culture.

Consider How You Work Positive . . .

. . . and consider how you can serve others through the unique contribution you make at work. Scan here to share online with the Work Positive Community #culturecounts

Small Acts of Huge Kindness

You have a unique contribution from which to serve others out of gratitude for the Work Positive culture you Receive. And yet there are some common pathways of service.

You have read story after story of random acts of kindness. The person at the drive-thru window who pays for the coffee of the person behind them, who then pays for the coffee of the next person, and so on for up to twenty-seven customers. The same type of generosity occurs at traffic toll booths.

You have done something similar. You held the door of a retail store for a person to wheel in. You let someone over into your lane of traffic. You arrived at a fast-food counter simultaneously with another parent and motioned the other parent ahead of you, remembering the challenges of eating out with an 18-month old.

There is so much kindness going around, particularly as you realize that while you Perceive, Conceive, Believe, and Achieve a Work Positive culture, more than anything else you Receive it.

Therefore, you serve others, knowing that what goes around comes around, you reap what you sow, all while motivated by an attitude of gratitude for how you Receive.

It is as you serve others who serve others that abundance displays brightly and the dark, negative work world lightens up. All the ships around you are lifted up on a rising Work Positive cultural tide and together, you and your teammates, boss, customers and suppliers work from a common hope. That which was impossible appears as possible.

We discover greatness as we serve each other.

Selfishness brings suffering. Service brings sustenance.

What goes around, comes around. You reap what you sow.

Receiving such service is a natural byproduct of how you create a Work Positive culture that attracts top talent and reduces team turnover so you increase productivity and profits. You Perceive and your positive thoughts expand. You Conceive and more positive people work with you as teammates and customers. You Believe and more resources converge than you imagined possible. You Achieve and more positive results appear than ever before.

Serve Others with Gratitude and Kindness

In *Love is the Killer App*, Tim Sanders tells the story of Tom Ward, CEO of Barton Protective Services. Tom was brought in to lead the company and turn the ship around.

One of the first things Tom did was to go on the road and visit all the local sales offices. He particularly enjoyed talking with Barton employees who were caught "doing something right." These women and men served their customers in a uniquely effective manner. Tom asked them to take a marker and draw him a map on a white board of how they did it. Tom honored the outstanding service of these employees by sharing their methods and giving them the credit. Barton then instituted these innovations in their customer relationships, offering the best service possible.

Such CEO-level service is rare, but evidently it pays huge dividends. Barton Protective Services was selected by Fortune as one of the Top 100 companies to work for, achieving that distinction four years running, and was the only security company ever selected. The company grew exponentially in revenue while lowering employee turnover and increasing customer retention. Tom Ward Works Positive because he serves others—customers and employees.

Together, serving one another in a company, you and your co-workers create a Work Positive culture.

Or, to put it another way, husbands serve their wives by selling shotguns to purchase baby cribs. Wives serve their husbands by buying shotguns back. And friends serve husbands and wives by giving the shotguns back.

Consider How You Work Positive . . .

Who can you serve right now? Think of one of your teammates who could use a reason to be grateful. What will you do? Think of one of your customers who could use a reason to be grateful. What will you do? When will you do these acts of gratitude for them? Scan here to share online with the Work Positive Community

#culturecounts

Grab & Go
"Serve Others" and:

1. Sell your shotgun to buy the crib. Watch as the shotgun returns.
2. Serve your customers and clients, co-workers and suppliers what they want instead of what you think they should have.
3. Serve your team members with an attitude of gratitude.
4. Love what you do for a living and use it to make a positive difference.
5. A rising tide lifts all ships . . . including yours.
6. The first shall be last and the last shall be first.
7. Together, serving one another, we create a Work Positive culture.

chapter 21

You Can Sustain Your Work Positive Culture

*"Few things in the world are more
powerful than a positive push."*
—Richard M. DeVos

ongratulations!
You design new neural pathways to Perceive how you create a Work Positive culture, discontent to dwell only in the Land of the Familiar ways to work. You choose to focus on the positive thoughts about work and filter out the negative mentally.

You now share your thoughts with other positive people, and collaborate in relationships of cooperation with them. You kicked a few Eeyore Vampires to the curb and Conceive the positive at work socially.

You claim your birthright to Believe emotionally that there is another reality in which you imagine your best work. You give no emotional energy to your ego, choosing to bend toward the best while you watch resources converge that exceed your imagination.

All of your efforts to Perceive mentally, Conceive socially, and Believe emotionally that you can create a Work Positive culture emerge in results that you Achieve physically. Your attention focuses on what is most important about work—positive thoughts and people—couple with the intentions you Believe, which propel you to act to Work Positive. You align your actions with your desires and strategically implement so the impossible is now possible.

Now you know how grateful you are for the many influences and people who gift you with successful work. Your gratitude spills over from the heart of your work into the lives of others as you squeeze yourself dry daily and serve others. When it's all said and done, you know that you Receive so much.

You now Work Positive.

How Will You Continue to Work Positive?

It's going to be anything except easy.

Continuing to create a Work Positive is the new challenge.

And that takes more than reading this book.

Remember the rubber band? How under no pressure, it lays there in your hand in one shape? But when you put it under pressure around that deck of cards, it takes on a whole new shape with a purpose?

You can continue to Work Positive once you put this book down, but it takes regular, consistent inspiration, instruction, and encouragement in the negative work world.

Negativity will creep back in, like fog, as you close this book. Slowly at first. Almost imperceptibly. But count on it—the negative work world will try to wedge back.

So, what can you do to continue to Work Positive? To receive regular, consistent inspiration, instruction, and encouragement?

You know how your doctor goes to classes to stay up to date on the latest techniques and treatments?

And how your CPA is required to do hours of continuing education to stay abreast of the latest tax law changes?

Your insurance agent must complete a certain number of units of education annually?

Consistent reinforcement of the five core practices of your Work Positive culture is necessary to keep you moving forward. Here's how you continue to create a Work Positive culture:

- **7 Keys to Work Positive Coaching Program**
  Dig deeper into each core practice of the Work Positive framework. Access online videos, specific action steps, and a collection of activities that build your Work Positive culture. Available for individuals and teams.
- **Work Positive Manager Coach Training**
  Transform your managers into coaches that create a positive work culture which attracts top talent and reduces team turnover. Increase productivity and profits with on-your-own video learning, live session training, along with demonstration and practice coaching rooted in the five core practices of a Work Positive culture.
- **Work Positive Team Tools**
  Sustain and develop your teams' Work Positive culture. Get a weekly podcast with specific action steps and guided activities that empower manager coaches to lead their teams to increase productivity and profits. Attract top talent and reduce team turnover with consistent, habit-driven positive culture tools.

- **Executive Coaching**

  Create a positive work culture with 1-2-1 coaching that proves its ROI across all industries. You select the Work Positive-certified coach most compatible with your values and needs. Or, work directly with culture architects Dr. Joey and Jane Creswell. Your coach. Your culture.

Are you ready to Perceive, Conceive, Believe, Achieve, and Receive your Work Positive culture so you attract top talent, reduce team turnover, and create a positive work culture that increases productivity and profits.

Go to WorkPositive.Today and start now.

The Next Years

"Learn to enjoy every minute of your life. Be happy now. Don't wait for something outside of yourself to make you happy in the future. Think how really precious is the time you have to spend, whether it's at work or with your family. Every minute should be enjoyed and savored."
—Earl Nightingale

So, now you know.

You know enough to pivot from "dissatisfied" to "satisfied" when asked how much you enjoy your work.

You know enough to redeem 70% of your waking hours spent at work and move from misery to magnificent.

You know enough to begin to create a Work Positive culture.

Yes, you know enough to transform your current work culture and invite others to join you.

And all of you together can help all of your teammates, customers, and suppliers to pivot and Work Positive.

Now imagine with me what this preferred future looks like beyond the work culture. The one consistent experience all of us share is work. What happens at work rarely stays at work.

This preferred future looks like a driver decelerating to allow a fellow driver to change lanes safely. Both drivers value life more than road rage.

It looks like middle-schoolers supporting each other instead of bullying. School children value each other more than suicide.

It looks like recovering addicts walking alongside active addicts to discover coping skills to deal with the harsh realities of the negative world. One beggar tells another beggar where to find sobriety.

You and I make a colossal mistake when we wait for COVID to finally go away or the economy to improve or the CEO to wake up and realize she can help transform the work culture.

The time at work and home is precious.

Start today—right now—to enjoy every minute of your life, especially the 70% of the waking hours you work.

And watch as the world around you transforms.

Top talent joins your teams.

Team members stay.

You create a positive work culture that increases productivity and profits.

Do it. Now.

The time at work and home is precious.

Work Positive in a negative world starting today.

acknowledgments

Tens of thousands of readers bought, read, and implemented the five core practices shared in the first edition of this book. So many, in fact, that it was a best-seller in multiple categories a dozen or so times. So, I must thank you, the readers, for embracing that book so enthusiastically which gave me the courage to write this Team Edition and include what I've learned since 2011 about how to Work Positive and the immense value of managers and teams in culture transformation. I am especially grateful for David Hancock, Jim Howard, and the rest of the incredible team at Morgan James Publishing for our positive collaboration as our publishing partner. Your culture is certainly Work Positive! Our friendship is equally amazing.

Rowan Cooley Faucette, my partner in all things, is the most incredible woman I could have ever talked into marrying me. Thank you for believing in me when my faith in myself sagged. You inspire me!

Jane Creswell, my partner in coaching companies to attract top talent, reduce team turnover and create a positive work culture that increases productivity and profits is a true gift who is more than I could ever imagine or request. I am grateful for you, sis!

The Work Positive Coach Community consists of the most gifted, skilled, and fun-loving coaches you can find anywhere on the planet. I celebrate each of you!

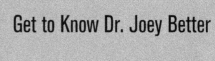

A certified executive coach and culture architect, Dr. Joey is a prolific writer of over 1,000 articles, eight books, and host of the Work Positive Podcast.

Since writing his first book in 2001, Dr. Joey has appeared as a guest on hundreds of podcasts and radio and TV shows across North America in most major markets. His company's website, WorkPositive.Today, reaches people in more than fifty countries.

He and his wife have two adult daughters and sons-in-law, the most brilliant and beautiful granddaughter ever born, four grand-dogs, and enjoy living on Pleasant Gap Farm with their yellow Lab—Maggie Mae, one horse, Bishop, and two cats—Boo Radley and Atticus Finch.

LinkedIn: https://www.linkedin.com/in/drjoeyfaucette/

Additional Work Positive Resources

Resources that empower your team to Work Positive.
Go to WorkPositive.Today and start today!

Download Book Bonuses

Thank you for purchasing the *Work Positive in a Negative World: The Team Edition* book. Download these bonuses that further empower you to create a Work Positive culture. Scan the QR code to get yours now!

- **Work Positive Checklist** – a simple checklist that coaches you to attract top talent and reduce team turnover.
- **Work Positive 5 Core Practices Cheat Sheet** – use this easy-to-follow guide to implement the 5 habit-sets of the Work Positive framework.
- **Work Positive Grab & Go Inspirations** – quick read positive thoughts to start your day in the best mindset.
- **Work Positive Affirmations** – begin each day the Work Positive way. Listen as Dr. Joey shares positive affirmations to focus on the positive and filter out the negative.

Join the Work Positive Community

Each of the "Consider How You Work Positive . . . " coaching box questions in this book are topics in the Work Positive Community online. You get a free membership with this book. Answer the questions online, learn from others' answers, and comment on them. Learn from the Work Positive Community how you can create a positive work culture that increases productivity and profits. Scan the QR code to set up your free account.

Discover More Work Positive Resources at WorkPositive.Today

- **7 Keys to Work Positive Coaching Program**
  Dig deeper into each core practice of the Work Positive framework. Access online videos, specific action steps, and a collection of activities that build your Work Positive culture. Available for individuals and teams.
- **Work Positive Manager Coach Training**
  Transform your managers into coaches that create a positive work culture which attracts top talent and reduces team turnover. Increase productivity and profits with on-your-own video learning, live session training, along with demonstration and practice coaching rooted in the five core practices of a Work Positive culture.
- **Work Positive Team Tools**
  Sustain and develop your teams' Work Positive culture. Get a weekly podcast with specific action steps and guided

activities that empower manager coaches to lead their teams to increase productivity and profits. Attract top talent and reduce team turnover with consistent, habit-driven positive culture tools.

- **Executive Coaching**
  Create a positive work culture with 1-2-1 coaching that proves its ROI across all industries. You select the Work Positive-certified coach most compatible with your values and needs. Or, work directly with culture architects Dr. Joey and Jane Creswell. Your coach. Your culture.

Printed in the USA
CPSIA information can be obtained
at www.ICGtesting.com
JSHW021042191223
53963JS00005B/338

9 781631 951350